ALEKSANDR CHAYANOV AND RUSSIAN BERLIN

T0347247

THE LIBRARY OF PEASANT STUDIES

Aleksandr Chayanov and Russian Berlin

Edited by

FRANK BOURGHOLTZER

FRANK CASS
LONDON • PORTLAND, OR

First published in 1999 in Great Britain by
FRANK CASS PUBLISHERS
Newbury House, 900 Eastern Avenue,
London IG2 7HH, England

and in the United States of America by
FRANK CASS PUBLISHERS
5804 N.E. Hassalo Street
Portland, Oregon 97213-3644

Transferred to Digital Printing 2004

Website: www.frankcass.com

Copyright © 1999 Frank Cass & Co. Ltd.

British Library Cataloguing in Publication Data

Aleksandr Chayanov and Russian Berlin. – (the library of
peasant studies ; no. 19)
1. Chaianov, A. (Aleksandr), 1888–1939 – Correspondence
2. Peasantry – Germany – Berlin – History 3. Russians –
Germany – Berlin – History
I. Bourgholtzer, Frank
305.5'633'0943155

ISBN 0 7146 5024 2 (cloth)
ISBN 0 7146 8080 X (paper)
ISSN 1462-219X

Library of Congress Cataloging in Publication Data

Chaianov, A. V. (Aleksandr Vasil'evich), 1888–1939.
    [Correspondence. Selections. English]
    Aleksandr Chayanov and Russian Berlin / edited by Frank
Bourgholtzer.
    p. cm.
    First appeared in a special issue of The journal of peasant
studies, v. 26/4 (July 1999).
    Includes bibliographical references (p.).
    ISBN 0-7146-5024-2 (cloth)
    ISBN 0-7146-8080-X (pbk.)
    1. Chaianov, A. V. (Aleksandr Vasil'evich), 1888–1939
Correspondence.   2. Economists–Soviet Union–Correspondence.   3.
Agriculture–Economic aspects–Soviet Union.   4. Peasantry–Soviet
Union.   I. Bourgholtzer, Frank, 1919–   II. Journal of peasant
studies. Special issue.   III. Title.
    HB113.C43 A4 1999
    330'.092–dc21
    [B]   99-34317
                                                              CIP

This group of studies first appeared in a Special Issue on
'Aleksandr Chayanov and Russian Berlin' of *The Journal of Peasant Studies*
(ISSN 0306 6150) Vol.26/4 (July 1999) published by Frank Cass.

Contents

List of Illustrations

Chayanov's wife, Ol'ga, is kneeling behind the two boys, Nikita on the left and Vasilii on the right. The identity of the second woman is not known: she is probably a neighbour in the *dacha* community. Nikita (born 1 May 1923) and Vasilii (born 20 February 1925) were in the army during the Second World War. Nikita was wounded and died of his wounds. Vasilii, who remained in the army for several years after the end of the war, had a career in cybernetics in the Soviet Union. He was kind enough to supply this and the following photograph.

These were the seminars that developed into his Agricultural Institute. Chayanov is seated in the front row. Behind Chayanov is Forunatov, directly to his right is Minin and furthest to the right in the third row appears to be Chelinstev.

Aleksei Fedorovich Fortunatov (1856–1925) was one of Chayanov's most influential teachers. Aleksandr Nikoforovich Minin (1881–1943) was a major player in Russia's co-operative movement and a close friend to Chayanov, presumably reflected in the character of the same name in 'Journey of My Brother ...'. Aleksandr Nikolaevich Chelintsev (1874–1962) taught at the Timiryazevskii Academy and was one of the founders of the 'Organization-Production School'.

Also known as the Yusupov Palace, it was built and rebuilt several times. Volkov, who was a deputy of A.D. Menshikov, occupied it in 1727, and was followed by Count G.A. Yusupov. The structure was reconstructed in 1870 and 1890.

It was just one street away from Chayanov's boyhood home. Chayanov wanted his Scientific Research Institute for Agrarian Economy and Agrarian Policy to be housed there. He succeeded in this after his return from Europe in 1923.

Page 10
Chayanov in 1924.

Page 11
Hildenborough as it looked around the time of Chayanov's stay at 3 New Council Cottages. Chayanov spent at least four months in Hildenborough in 1922.

Page 12
The editor, Frank Bourgholtzer, working on various 'Top Secret' papers relating to Chayanov in Yuri Andropov's Conference Room, in the Lubyanka, in the first week of July 1991.

Foreword

One of the frustrations encountered in seeking to view the results of agrarian research on Russia of the decades before and after 1930 has been the absence of much relevant material, as a result of political confiscation in the period of Joseph Stalin. Through the efforts, verging upon the heroic, of such investigators as Basile Kerblay, Daniel Thorner, R.E.F. Smith and Teodor Shanin, many lost documents have been found and reconstituted. An important degree of scientific rehabilitation has resulted, especially in the case of the pioneer theorist Alexander Vasilievich Chayanov. This study, edited and presented by Frank Bourgholtzer, deals with some aspects of Chayanov's life and work hitherto unknown, during the period, in the early 1920s, when he wrote some of his most significant work, on the central theme of the theory of peasant economy. He was, at that time, living outside of Russia. He was in constant contact with his long-time mentor, colleague and critic, Sergei Nikolaevich Prokopovich, also living abroad at that time. Their environment was emigrant Germany, when Berlin was the 'Third Capital' of Russia. They discussed, agreed on, and disagreed on the work that each of them was doing. At the same time, Chayanov was writing two novellas of fantastic fiction, collecting and writing about old engravings, organising publication in Germany of the work of his Russian colleagues, not to mention worrying about the birth of his and his wife's first child. Details of these aspects of both his mundane and his creative life have become available in a series of letters that he wrote, letters which offer a certain perspective to students of Chayanov's work, and which are the foundation of this special issue of *The Journal of Peasant Studies*. It consists of an Introduction by Terence J. Byres, a substantial essay on 'Alexander Chayanov and Russian Berlin' by Frank Bourgholtzer, 41 letters, an Appendix on 'Chayanov and Socialist Agriculture' and a comprehensive Biographical Glossary.

Acknowledgements

The present essay is a result of a quest that began in Moscow in the 1980s, a journalistic investigation, a search for the true sources of the economic reforms proposed by Mikhail Gorbachev. Guided by Nikolai Shishlin, the politician, Abel Aganbegyan, the economist, and Moshe Lewin, the historian, who was in Moscow at the time, doing his own research, my first target became V.S. Nemchinov, and the Timiryazevskii Agricultural Academy.

Olga Nikolayevna Bychkova, the gentle librarian at Timiryazevskii, informed me about Nemchinov and then, having done her duty, urged me to inspect also a special exhibit about a predecessor of Nemchinov's, a certain victim of Stalinist repression who had just been rehabilitated, Aleksandr Vasilievich Chayanov. At that moment, the journalistic quest acquired a new focus, a new goal: to find the reality of this nearly-forgotten figure, his work, his personality, his significance.

His surviving son, Vasilii Aleksandrovich, authorised me to approach the 'G.B.' the security forces that had buried not only Chayanov, but his record. In the volumes of the interrogation, with due account for the fact that his 'confessions' were written at the command of an inquisitor, Chayanov had created what amounted to his only autobiography. Once I had a copy of this text, Vasilii Aleksandrovich helped me to understand it. He was later permitted to take my transcript back to the G.B. for verification and correction, where necessary.

Finding and evaluating the sometimes tiny bits of information, and fitting them together into something approaching a comprehensive picture, called for much help from many, many helpers. To name a few — Konstantin Georgiev Nasonov, the G.B. officer who conducted the scrupulous examination of the entire Chayanov record to substantiate the crimes that had been committed against him, and the grounds for his rehabilitation; Vladimir Goncharev, the G.B. agent who kept tabs on me as I perused the 'top secret' Chayanov record, working in the spacious room that had been Yurii Andropov's conference room; Yurii Ivanovich Oshibkin, the G.B. agent who produced the secret records and arranged my work sessions. Extraordinary assistance was provided by Irina Ovchasova, who worked with me and managed to come away with a word-for-word copy of the Chayanov record despite the prohibition against making photocopies.

Later, Vasilii Aleksandrovich shared with me a number of letters that his father had written from England and Germany, 1922–23, letters that are the basis of this special issue/book. My investigation of the letters called for innumerable consultations with Vasilii Aleksandrovich, using both ordinary and electronic mail. Vital to this communication were Natasha Gromova and Lyuba Ovchintseva, as well as Vasilii's grand-daughter, Svetlana. At crucial moments, Professor John Whitely of the University of California in Irvine generously helped to expedite my communications. Professor Viktor Danilov of Moscow's Inercentre shared his knowledge of documents still missing from Chayanov's biography. Dr Phillipp Gerhardt, at Michigan State University, provided useful material about Nikolai Kondrat'ev, as did Kondrat'ev's daughter, Elena Kondrat'eva. Katya Rozhdestvensky helped in the study of Russian texts. Uwe Junghanns in Leipzig helped us to locate the town of Schreiberhau. Alan Brooke Turner, a Moscow veteran, also helped greatly in the search for Chayanov's residence in Hildenborough, as did Ted and Joan Dash. Librarians everywhere have been patient, knowledgeable, and wonderful. This was especially true of Carol Leadenham and Molly Molloy at Stanford, of Ellen Scaruffi and Tanya Chebotarev at Columbia, and of Karen Rondestvedt at the University of Pittsburgh.

Among those who have been generous in advice and insightful comments on the Chayanov material were Vladimir Bronislavovich Muraviev, discussing Chayanov's literary life, and Voldemar Nikolaevich Balyazin, who shared his biographical knowledge of Chayanov. Evgeniya Viktorovna Serova, as a scholar and agronomist involved in the current development of agriculture in Russia, was especially helpful in discussion of Chayanov's work and activities. Vadim Golovanov and Viktor Louis provided useful guidance on the subject of the Security Organs and their operatives.

In the development of the essay, Shena McLaren was a vigilant assistant at every stage of the process. Professor E. Paul Durrenberger was enthusiastically encouraging, and put me in touch with Professor James Scott, who read an early version and recommended it to Henry Bernstein. Tom Brass challenged it where it needed to be challenged and offered suggestions where it needed improvement. His contribution was very important.

Professor Terence J. Byres has been the ultimate editor, understanding what the essay could and should convey, and guiding the author with tremendous patience, skill and insight. The result, to the degree that it has merit, has merit because of Terry Byres.

Frank Bourgholtzer
April 1999

1

Editor's Introduction

TERENCE J. BYRES

This special issue, edited and presented by Frank Bourgholtzer, continues *The Journal of Peasant Studies* tradition of scholarship relating to the ideas of Alexander Vasilevich Chayanov (1888–1937). Here it is Chayanov of the early 1920s who receives attention: through the medium of letters hitherto unpublished in English. There are 41 letters in the collection: 39 from Chayanov, one from Maxim Gorky (to Ekaterina Kuskova) and one from Ekaterina Kuskova (to Vera Figner). These are introduced in an essay by Frank Bourgholtzer, entitled 'Alexander Chayanov and Russian Berlin', which sets the letters in the context of the Russian émigré community in Berlin of the early 1920s – the capital of émigré Russia of the time, the so-called 'Third Capital of Russia' – and provides a sympathetic treatment of Chayanov. Bourgholtzer provides, too, an extensive Biographical Glossary, relating to those many individuals who appear in the text. In addition, an Appendix on Chayanov's planned work of the early 1920s on socialist agriculture is published.

The *JPS* tradition of scholarship on Alexander Chayanov started in the early days of the journal, with an important article by Mark Harrison on 'Chayanov and the Economics of the Russian Peasantry' [*Harrison*, 1975]. This was followed by the publication, in 1976, in a special issue edited by R.E.F. Smith, of the first English translation of Chayanov's remarkable utopian novel, *The Journey of my Brother Alexei to the Land of Peasant*

Terence J. Byres, Department of Economics, School of Oriental and African Studies, University of London, Thornhaugh Street, Russell Square, London, WC1H OXG. E-mail tbl@soas.ac.uk

Utopia [*Smith*, 1977]. That was a notable event. The novel was written by Chayanov during the period of 'War Communism' (1918–21), and published in 1920, under the pseudonym Ivan Kremnev. It opens in October 1921, and is set in a de-urbanised Moscow of 1984, 50 years after a peasant counter-revolution had taken place in 1934. As Bourgholtzer has it : 'In his imaginary 1984, Russia had achieved a totally co-operative form of economic organization, led by a peasant-dominated government'. Or, as Smith described the novel, it is 'an imagined realisation of peasant socialism' [1977: 7].

As Bourgholtzer stresses, Chayanov himself tended to classify it as one of his scientific works, and regarded it as one of the four most important works of 'theory' which he wrote on the peasantry in the period 1917–22. Certainly, the essence of Chayanovian theory of the peasantry, and of his vision of how a suitably reconstituted peasant society might function in a modern setting, are captured brilliantly there. It receives considerable attention in this special issue, and new light is cast upon it: on how Chayanov conceived it; on his nervousness about his identity as its author being found out by the new Soviet authorities. Certainly, his anxiety would later be justified, when the novel was seen as a blueprint for an anti-Soviet counter-revolution, and he was arrested, imprisoned, and ultimately shot: events that Bourgholtzer details.

In addition to the foregoing, we have published in the *JPS* a number of further papers on Chayanov by Harrison [1977a, 1977b, 1979], and papers by Hunt [1979] and Patnaik [1979]; while Chayanov's ideas have been seriously addressed in other contributions to the journal (for example, by Byres [1979]). *The Journal of Peasant Studies* can hardly be said to have ignored Chayanov. If some of that treatment has been critical, it has always been based upon serious recognition of the importance of Chayanov's ideas.

Here Frank Bourgholtzer carries forward our knowledge and understanding of Chayanov: as person and scholar; as theorist of the peasantry and as bellelettrist; the Chayanov who pursued his ideas on the peasantry not merely in empirical studies and theoretically, but via the novel and film. We have noted his utopian novel. Bourgholtzer brings to our attention the film about agriculture for which Chayanov in 1928 wrote the screenplay and which he produced – *Albidum (Victory over the Sun)*. His 'hero' was an agricultural scientist, developing a revolutionary theory for the production of grain, working against time to produce a large crop for export; with the grain triumphantly loaded aboard a ship bound for foreign markets in the film's climax. As with his novel, so in the film the Chayanovian view of the peasantry is deployed creatively and to imaginative effect. As Bourgholtzer points out in the Biographical Glossary, Rashit Marvanovich Yangirov has published in the magazine *Kinostsenarii* (No. 5, 1989) the text of Chayanov's film script, with an accompanying text in which he gives an account of the filming and a biography of Chayanov (see the Yangirov entry).

Certainly, this special issue makes possible a far more rounded view of Chayanov than we have had previously in English. It evokes the atmosphere in which he lived and worked. It communicates the circumstances of his family life, explores his friendships, and reveals the remarkable variety of his interests. It provides, indeed, valuable new insight into Chayanov's ideas and the milieu in which he developed them in the 1920s. We may highlight some of the further ways in which Bourgholtzer adds to our knowledge and understanding of Chayanov.

The first is that, while Smith could speculate that 'Chayanov himself ... appears to have been in England in 1922' [1977: 10], Bourgholtzer gives precise information on the circumstances of Chayanov's stay of six months, in that year, in England. At least four months of that period were spent in the village of Hildenborough, in Kent, and we publish here letters written by Chayanov from Hildenborough. He arrived in England in April, and left on 28 October.

Secondly, hitherto there has been some vagueness as to what precisely *neonarodism* signified for Chayanov. It was, after all, a term of abuse used by his detractors, which he was most likely either to ignore or reject. Here we have a clear definition of what *neonarodism* meant for him: all the more poignant, perhaps, inasmuch as it was given to his secret police interrogator, Agranov, as part of a 'confession', yet resolute and uncompromising. *Neonarodism*, he told his interrogator, was 'a theory for the development of agriculture on the basis of cooperative peasant households, a peasantry organized cooperatively as an independent class and technically superior to all other forms of agricultural organization'. That is as clear and cogent a definition as one could wish for.

Thirdly, we gain some insight, if only briefly, into the ambivalent relationship between Chayanov and his colleague Nikolai Dmitrievich Kondrat'ev (1892–1938), a brilliant economist, of considerable and varied accomplishment, and best-known in the West for his work on the trade cycle, his theory of long cycles (on Kondrat'ev see, for example, Jasny [1972: 158–78] and Schumpeter [1954: 743, 1124, 1158]; and on more recent attempts to test his theories Solomou [1988] and Mandel [1980]). Kondrat'ev was one of the closest of M.I. Tugan-Baranovsky's pupils: Tugan-Baranovsky, according to Jasny, 'the greatest Russian economist of all time' [1972: 158–9] . Jasny describes Kondrat'ev as 'the leader of the neo-narodniks' [1972: 158] in the 1920s. Chayanov invited him to set up a Conjuncture Institute when he established his Institute for the Study of Economics and Agrarian Policy in Moscow in 1919. This Kondrat'ev did in 1920, and it 'played a great role in the ensuing decade' [*Jasny*, 1972: 163]. We find Chayanov, during his absence abroad, worrying whether his gifted young colleague, the de facto Director of the Institute for the Study of Economics and Agrarian Policy during Chayanov's sojourn in Europe, might be usurping his position at the Institute. At one point, Chayanov asks sarcastically whether Kondrat'ev had really been made a 'professor' or whether he was signing 'prof' under his name, in the *Economic Bulletin of the Conjuncture Institute*, merely 'because of naive vanity'. The Academy, it seems, has certain universal attributes.

Fourthly, our knowledge of Chayanov's relationship with Marxism has hitherto been vague and insubstantial, to be inferred in oppositional terms, so to speak, rather than stated concretely. That relationship does not emerge at all clearly from his writing that already exists in English [1966, 1977, 1991]. Here it is clarified, somewhat at least, with respect to one tendency in Russian Marxism: its revisionist wing, that of Legal Marxism (whose major exponents included M.I. Tugan-Baranovsky, P.B. Struve, N.A. Berdyaev, S.N. Bulgakov and S.L. Frank). That clarification comes via the account given of Chayanov's close, but ultimately ruptured, friendship with Sergei Nikolaevich Prokopovich (1871–1955). Prokopovich was a lifelong Marxist who, as Legal Marxist, attracted the powerful criticism of Lenin (from 1899 onwards). He would remain in permanent exile from June 1922. Prokopovich was Chayanov's senior by some 17 years. Chayanov received his diploma from the Moscow Agricultural Institute in February, 1911, and immediately joined the department headed by Prokopovich, for the study of co-operatives (see Chayanov [1991: Danilov's introduction, xxi-xxii]; and Balyazin [1990: 48–9]). Chayanov, at that time, taught also at the Popular University in Moscow, the Shanyanvskii University (a course on 'Geography and History of Agricultural Life'), along with Prokopovich, and others who included M.I. Tugan-Baranovsky. Prokopovich and Chayanov shared a passion for the cooperative movement, became friends and had constant intellectual exchange. They developed teaching techniques together; Prokopovich read and commented on Chayanov's work; and Chayanov relied upon Prokopovich's statistical expertise. The grounds on which their ideas proved incompatible, and how this came to a head, are given fascinating treatment in what follows. That treatment illuminates something of Chayanov's relationship with Marxism.

The fifth fascinating addition to our knowledge is contained in the Appendix, which reproduces Chayanov's letter to the secret police, of 21 June 1931, in which he outlines the plan of work he first began to pursue in the early 1920s on 'Calculations and Methods of Determining the Effectiveness of Socialist Agriculture and Farming'. Here, a closer engagement with Marxist methodology and ideas is revealed than we see anywhere else in Chayanov's writing (at least that available in English); while Chayanov's serious efforts to confront the problems of socialist agriculture are revealed. It would be most valuable to have published in English the works of 1920 and 1929–30 to which Chayanov refers (the works published in Russian of 1920 and 1929–30 are identified in the 'Bibliography of A.V. Chayanov' which appears in Chayanov [1966]). We must thank Frank Bourgholtzer for reminding us of that.

We are grateful to Jim Scott and Tom Brass: the former for directing Frank Bourgholtzer towards *The Journal of Peasant Studies* and the latter for some preliminary editorial work on this special issue.

REFERENCES

Balyazin, V.N., 1990, *Professor Aleksandr Chayanov*, Moskva: Agropromizdat.
Byres, Terence J., 1979, 'Of Neo-Populist Pipe Dreams: Daedalus in the Third World and the Myth of Urban Bias', *Journal of Peasant Studies*, Vol.6, No.2, Jan., pp.210–44.
Chayanov, A.V., 1966, *The Theory of Peasant Economy*, Homewood, IL: Richard Irwin for the American Economic Association, 1966), edited by Daniel Thorner, Basile Kerblay and R.E.F. Smith. See also the 1986 reprint with a New Introduction by Teodor Shanin, Madison, WI: University of Wisconsin Press.
Chayanov, A.V., 1977, *The Journey of my Brother Alexei to the Land of Peasant Utopia*, in Smith [1977: 63–108]. First published in Russian in 1920, by the State Publishing House, Moscow.
Chayanov, Alexander, 1991, *The Theory of Peasant Cooperatives*, London and New York: I.B. Tauris.
Harrison, Mark, 1975, 'Chayanov and the Economics of the Russian Peasantry', *The Journal of Peasant Studies*, Vol.2, No.4, July, pp.389–417.
Harrison, Mark, 1977a, 'Resource Allocation and Agrarian Class Formation',The *Journal of Peasant Studies*, Vol.4, No.2, Jan., pp.127–61.
Harrison, Mark, 1977b, 'The Peasant Mode of Production in the Work of A.V. Chayanov', *The Journal of Peasant Studies*, Vol.4, No.4, July, pp.323–36.
Harrison, Mark, 1979, 'Chayanov and the Marxists', *The Journal of Peasant Studies*,Vol.7, No.1, Oct., pp.86–100.
Hunt, Diana, 1979, 'Chayanov's Model of Peasant Household Resource Allocation', *The Journal of Peasant Studies*, Vol.6, No.3, April, pp.247–85.
Jasny, Naum, 1972, *Soviet Economists of the Twenties: Names to be Remembered*, Cambridge: Cambridge University Press.
Mandel, Ernest, 1980, *Long Waves of Capitalist Development: The Marxist Interpretation*, Cambridge and Paris: Cambridge University Press and Editions de la Maison des Sciences de l'Homme.
Patnaik, Utsa, 1979, 'Neo-Populism and Marxism: The Chayanovian View of the Agrarian

Question and Its Fundamental Fallacy', *The Journal of Peasant Studies*, Vol.6, No.4, July, pp.375–420.

Schumpeter, Joseph, 1954, *History of Economic Analysis*, London: George Allen & Unwin.

Smith, R.E.F. (ed.), 1977, *The Russian Peasant 1920 & 1984*, London: Frank Cass. (First published as a special issue of *The Journal of Peasant Studies*, Vol.4, No.1, Oct. 1976.)

Solomou, Solomos, 1988, *Phases of Economic Growth 1850–1973: Kondratieff Waves and Kuznets Swings*, Cambridge: Cambridge University Press.

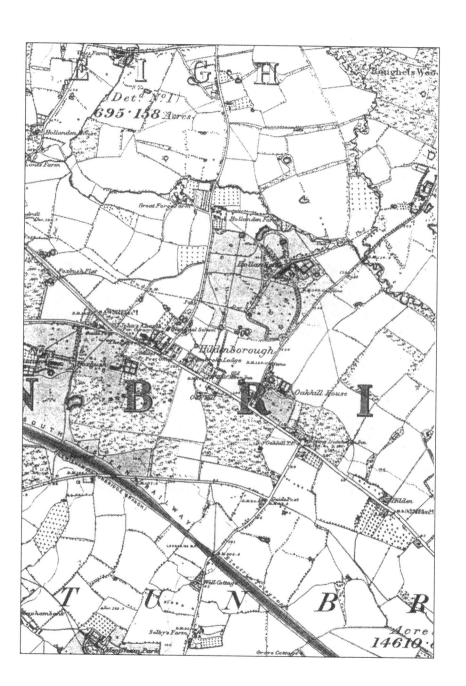

2

Aleksandr Chayanov and Russian Berlin

FRANK BOURGHOLTZER

Aleksandr Chayanov, in August of 1922, when he was living temporarily in a cottage in Hildenborough, Kent, wrote in a letter to his esteemed friend, Ekaterina Kuskova, about his plans for the coming year. They were, he said, plans of a 'strictly scientific character'. His goal was: '… to establish a scientific foundation for my basic social beliefs' [Letters, 6]. He went on to describe the exact nature of this scientific activity – the work with which his name would be most associated, during his lifetime and afterward.

'Concretely', he said, 'I have already succeeded in producing a rough draft of 3 large chapters of *Peasant Economy*.[1] I am working now on the 4th, and there are about 10 still to come.'

There was a clue in this letter, as well, to one aspect of his social beliefs. Kuskova had written that she planned to launch a newspaper in Berlin, and asked for Chayanov's advice. In response, he applauded her editorial policy: 'to transform the Russian problem from one of struggle against the régime to one of redemption and re-birth of the homeland, with all its existing forces, including the Communists – to the extent that they have a living, creative origin …'.

There is a paucity of information about Chayanov the man, about his daily life – how he worked, what he liked and did not like, what tickled his intellectual fancy, how he approached his scientific labours. The Stalinist repression not only cut short his life; it confiscated all his personal possessions, including his very large library, his papers, his notebooks, and his correspondence.[2]

Frank Bourgholtzer, 1702 Pine Street, Santa Monica, CA 90405, USA.

For the period during which he lived and worked in western Europe, there is almost no extant material that can be classified, even now, as autobiographical, other than that contained in portions of the two volumes of his interrogation by the Soviet Secret Police after his arrest in 1930, and in the texts of a small collection of letters that he wrote between April 1922 and October 1923, from England and Germany.[3]

These letters provide new insights into the intellectual/theoretical genesis of his ideas about peasant economy, about the dynamic of the family farm. They shed light on the place in his life occupied by his romantic tales, the stories that he wrote in admiration of E.T.A. Hoffman. They illuminate the political, social and economic atmosphere in which he lived, studied and wrote, when Berlin was briefly a world centre of art and letters, as well as the capital of émigré Russia, and when Bolshevik Russia was the world to which he, and all émigrés, had to consider returning.

He had serious doubts about returning. He disclosed them to Kuskova in the late summer of 1923 [Letters, 38], when he wrote that he felt impelled to devise 'fantastic ideas' for the future of his country, because 'I am working with all my strength, but, if there is no vista, then, involuntarily, I find myself thinking that I may be persuaded to transfer my agricultural work to somewhere else, perhaps to Lithuania, perhaps to Estonia.'

In 1930, he was arrested and imprisoned. In 1937, he was shot.

I

Ensconced in Lubyanka, Russia's most notorious prison, Chayanov had been led, on 25 August 1930, to confess to the chief of the Secret Department of the OGPU,[4] Yakov Agranov, writing by hand on incongruous scraps of blue paper, that he had been a 'Neonarodnik'. Narodism (Populism) was a heteromorphic word in the Russian political vocabulary. Its stigma for Chayanov went back to the mid-nineteenth century and Alexander Herzen, Russia's most influential revolutionary-in-exile. He had inspired the term, *Narodnik*, in 1861, in a message to students who were wondering where they should go after having been driven out of the University of St. Petersburg by Cossacks in the service of the Tsar. Where should they go? 'To the *Narod* (people)', said Herzen.

Since 85 per cent of Russia's people were peasants, going to the people meant going to the peasants. The *Zemstvos*, organs of local government, began 'going to the people' by sponsoring the collection of information about peasant farms, information that would allow them to understand and help the peasants. This peasant information also provided the type of statistical data on which Chayanov and his colleagues would later base their theories, but it was, in essence, *narodnik* behaviour.

Politically, the term 'Narodnik' was employed by a young revolutionary, Nikolai Tchaikovskii, in a campaign of education to prepare the peasants for a socialist revolution. Marxist theory, at the time, held that such a revolution could be successful only if it were built on a previous bourgeois revolution, Tchaikovskii came to the conclusion that Russia was different from the West, that its peasants would not need an intermediate bourgeois revolution. He was supported by Slavophiles, who also believed that Russia was unique and should not be influenced by Western thought.

The schism between *Narodniks* and Marxists came, however, on the question of terrorism. The most ardent *Narodniks* carried on a campaign of terrorism and assassination. A bright young Marxist, Georgi Plekhanov, who had taken part in *Narodnik* work with the peasants, decided that 'individual' terror was futile. He became the leader of a group that believed that the desired revolution could come about only by the actions of industrial workers. The *Narodnik* path would lead to disaster.

From this moment, Marxism – as practised by Plekhanov and his disciple, Lenin – became incompatible with Narodism. A 'Narodnik' was an enemy.

Chayanov could have been considered a *Narodnik* in the purest sense, since it was from his detailed examination of the people, their life on their family farms, that his fundamental theories evolved. But he did not see himself either as the violent activist the term had come to represent or as the 'Neonarodnik' his opponents had begun to call him.

For Bolsheviks, the term 'Neonarodnik' was a play on words, an extension of their historic opposition to *Narodniks*. It was first used against Chayanov, however, by one of his own colleagues, a non-Bolshevik, Lev Litoshenko, to express opposition to Chayanov's economic theories.[5] Young Bolshevik economists, who began to call themselves Agrarian Marxists, adopted the term to brand Chayanov as an enemy of Bolshevism. By 1930, Stalin, the leader of the Bolsheviks, had defined *Narodniks*, or *Neonarodniks*, as enemies of – 'the Narod'.

Documents such as Secret Police interrogations must be read with caution. One must recognise that the policeman will have required certain words to be stated in the confession, while the victim will have tried to meet these requirements and still express what he or she wanted to express.

'My invitation to join the staff of the Narkomzem R.S.F.S.R.[6] in 1921', Chayanov told Agranov during his interrogation in Lubyanka, 'in the very first weeks of the NEP[7] was brought about by Kuraev precisely because at that time I found myself in the full flower of enthusiasm for NeoNarodism' [*OGPU*, 10: 74–8].

This wording satisfied Agranov's requirement that Chayanov 'confess' to NeoNarodism. The same wording fulfilled Chayanov's own agenda, establishing for the record that the Bolsheviks had invited him to join their government precisely because he was a *Neonarodnik*. He went on to spell out his definition of his NeoCadet: 'a theory for the development of agriculture on the basis of cooperative peasant households, a peasantry organized cooperatively as an independent class and technically superior to all other forms of agricultural organization' [*OGPU*, 10: 75–8].

Agranov dutifully put it all in the archive.

The attraction that Chayanov had for the Bolsheviks in 1921 was his experience with the peasant economy. Vladimir Lenin and his fledgling government knew very little about running agriculture, running business or, for that matter, running a government. The country had to be rescued from 'War Communism', and Lenin's formula was a 'New Economic Policy'. As Zhores Medvedev [1987: 38] said of NEP, 'changing course was a matter of survival, not a question of wisdom'.

The co-operatives, in 1921, were virtually the only organs of trade and distribution in Russia that still functioned reasonably well, and Chayanov was a major figure in the co-operative movement. Before the first World War, he had teamed with Sergei Prokopovich to set up a university department for the study of cooperatives. This department, in the 'people's' Shanyavskii University,[8] quickly became the intellectual centre for co-operative development. Chayanov had organised one of the most successful co-operative ventures in Russia, the Linen Centre, and helped it to develop a successful export trade.

His series of high-level seminars on agricultural economics had become the basis of a new research institute.[9] Chayanov was director. The Institute, as part of the Petrovskii Agricultural Academy, was already Russia's leading scientific body dealing with agriculture. It became, in effect, an adjunct of the Commissariat of Agriculture, Narkomzem. Many of the young economists who would become Agrarian Marxists were among Chayanov's students. He also was active in the leadership of the Tsentrosoyuz (Central Association of Consumer Societies),[10] the organ that Commissar of Foreign Trade Leonid Krasin would preempt as a vehicle for bypassing the West's economic blockade of Russia. Scandinavian, French and British businessmen could not legally deal directly with the Russian government but they could deal with Tsentrosoyuz.[11]

When the Commissariat of Agriculture invited Chayanov to join its staff, he already was working for them, with several colleagues,[12] as an advisor on the most significant of the reforms that constituted the New Economic Policy, the so-called 'tax in kind' for agriculture.[13] This method of appropriating a percentage of the peasant's harvest seemed positively beneficent compared to the policy of outright confiscation that it replaced.[14] The confiscations had swept up entire harvests, including even the crops that were growing seed for the next year's planting.

The New Policy gave the Bolshevik leaders some breathing space, but it came too late to prevent one of the worst famines in Russia's history.

It became difficult in those harsh circumstances to put one's mind to such matters as the scientific calculation of coefficients of correlation for the agricultural income of a peasant farm in relation to the size and composition of the peasant family. The savage reality was that some peasant families, in 1921, were even driven to eating their new-born children for dinner, just to remain alive for a few more days.[15] Lenin used the New Economic Policy, and people like Chayanov, to hold peasant hostility at bay.

For Lenin, the Russian peasantry was socially differentiated. Lenin's rich peasant – the *kulak* – was an anti-social farmer-capitalist, motivated strictly by avarice, and predestined to play a capitalistic game of unseemly profiteering, hoarding grain and restricting production to drive up prices.

For Chayanov, such social differentiation was without significance. Chayanov's archetypal peasant, by contrast with Lenin's rich peasant, had a more primitive motivation: to work as long and as hard as necessary to satisfy the family's material needs; no longer, no harder. When the degree of material satisfaction to be obtained by one more day's work was not worth the drudgery of another day in the fields, the peasant would just stay at home. This concept of 'drudgery' set Chayanov's analysis apart from the main stream of economic thought.

It is possible that the notion of drudgery appealed to Chayanov, in part, because, unlike most of his fellow scientists, he also was a writer of fiction, of fanciful tales. He was accustomed to look for and follow the twists and turns of human motivation in terms of psychology, and emotion, as well as in terms of economics and politics. He had published, in 1920, under a pseudonym [*Kremnev*, 1920], a little book of scientific fantasy entitled *The Journey of my Brother Alexei to the Land of the Peasant Utopia*. In it, he had projected an idealistic Russia that, in the year 1984, would be a Socialist, but non-Communist land of plenty. In Chayanov's fantasy, the Communists had lost power in the mid-1930s. In his imaginary 1984, Russia had achieved a totally co-operative form of economic organisation, led by a peasant-dominated government. This fantasy would eventually get Chayanov into all sorts of trouble with staid Bolsheviks, who classified his story as a blueprint for an anti-Soviet counter-revolution rather than an exercise in 'what if?' fiction, playing out his concept of co-operative development supported by radical scientific achievement.[16]

The Russian economy of 1920 was in chaos, but, at the same time, in that first quarter of the twentieth century, there had been a 'Silver Age' of the arts and sciences that lingered on even after the Bolshevik revolution. It was a time of inspired poetry, music, art, theatre, literature, a time of scientific innovation that encompassed not only Russia, but all of Europe, east and west. For a brief period in the early 1920s, this surge of creativity would make Berlin the arts centre of the world that Paris had been, and would again become. Chayanov did not know it in 1920, but he, along with thousands of other Russians, was headed for Berlin.

II

Two friends who also were destined to take part in the Berlin scene were Sergei Prokopovich, and Prokopovich's wife, Ekaterina Kuskova, a prominent publicist, editor of the implacably anti-Bolshevik newspaper, *Vlast Naroda* (The People's Power). Their passage to Berlin would be a direct result of their humanitarian effort to do something to assuage the appalling famine of 1921–22.

In that period, according to one historian, Dmitri Volkoganov, [1994b: 207], 25 million Russians were starving. The agricultural scientist Zhores Medvedev [1987: 40] reports that more than five million people died of malnutrition and starvation in the winter of 1921–22.' The Great Soviet Encyclopedia [*Encyclopedia*: 463] refers to 35 gubernia with a total population of 90 million stricken by the famine in 1921–22, with 'no fewer than 35 million starving at that time'. For the Bolsheviks, it was a political disaster. Lenin feared, with reason, that the proletarian masses, if he could not feed them, would turn on him. Foreign assistance seemed to be out of the question because western countries refused to recognise Lenin's government and had no interest in helping it to survive.

This political threat led Lenin to accept, provisionally, an offer of assistance from Kuskova, Prokopovich and a group of non-Bolshevik intellectuals. They proposed to use their influence abroad to attract help for the suffering population. The resulting 'All-Russian Committee to Aid the Hungry' succeeded in focusing world-wide attention on the Russian famine.

Ironically, the Committee's very success led to its downfall. One of its members, Maksim Gorkii, sent a telegram [*Fischer,* 1964: 601–2] asking for help from Herbert Hoover, then running the American Relief Administration. Hoover replied immediately, and his minions proceeded to make a deal directly with the Soviet government, bypassing the All-Russian Committee.

That allowed Lenin to dissolve the All-Russian Committee forthwith and order the arrest of its non-Bolshevik members. Kuskova, Prokopovich and four others were condemned to death [*Heller,* 1991].

Chayanov had been a member of the Committee. Presumably because of his position in the Agriculture Commissariat, he was not arrested. He had, in fact, been assigned, on 7 October, to represent the Commissariat at meetings with the planning organ, Gosplan. He was trying to deal with the famine from inside Lenin's government.

He worked to build a network of provincial agricultural organisations; he prepared a new decree on co-operatives; and he organised a campaign to plant 11 million poods of winter seeds. He served on the praesidium of an emergency 'Economic Conference' that met for ten days every month from May to December; to discuss everything from a plan for the next year's operation of the Commissariat to a global plan for the total reorganisation of Russian agriculture.[17] He began to assemble documentation on the subject of concessions that might be offered to Western business firms, as a means of building the Soviet economy.

Somehow, in addition to all his official activities, Chayanov found time to publish scholarly works, among them a 'Study of the Isolated State' [*Chayanov,* 1921], and a treatise on the 'Optimal Size of an Agricultural Enterprise' [*Chayanov,* 1922]. Together with his colleague, Gennadii Studenskii, he published a 'History of Budgetary Research' [*Chayanov,* 1922]. With his close friend, and cousin, Sokrat Klepikov, he edited a 'Statistical Reference Book on the Agrarian Question' [*Chayanov and Klepikov (red.),* 1922].

The death sentences against Prokopovich and Kuskova were modified to internal exile, at the urgent request of Fridtjof Nansen.[18] Prokopovich and Kuskova were sent to Vologda, a northern region where Prokopovich had carried out some of his most extensive statistical studies of peasant budgets. After a vain attempt to make habitable the tumbledown house to which they were assigned in exile, they were transferred to Kazan, a city in the valley of the Volga, wracked with starvation and typhus. On their way to Kazan, they met friends who helped them to settle, instead, in the little village of Kashin, near Tver, where they would remain until June of 1922.

Chayanov's road to Berlin was inextricably linked to the activities of Leonid Borisovich Krasin, the charismatic Russian engineer who had been Lenin's close ally in the earliest years of the Bolshevik Party, had turned his back on Lenin to become a successful businessman working for the captains of capitalism in Germany and Russia, then had returned to Moscow to rejoin Lenin and his revolution. [*O'Connor*, 1992: 123–38]. Krasin became the chief patron of the *spetsy*, the non-party specialists like Chayanov who could make the New Economic Policy work, and he believed passionately that the economic salvation of the revolution lay in an infusion of western capital by means of economic concessions. He tried to convince Lenin that, if western capitalists had profitable concessions in Russia, there would be no need for Russia to fear anything like armed intervention from abroad.

Beginning in March of 1921, he had done everything in his power to forge a major agreement with the English tycoon, John Leslie Urquhart, whose Russo-Asiatic Consolidated Corporation had operated huge concessions in Siberia before the war. In October, however, Urquhart had to tell Krasin that the deal was off because of disagreements over a handful of clauses in the contract. Krasin and Urquhart did not give up. They simply bided their time. A major world summit conference on economic questions, engineered by the British Prime Minister Lloyd George and Krasin, was going to be held in Genoa, Italy.

Chayanov was engrossed in preparations for that Genoa conference, and he was concentrating on proposals for agricultural concessions. At the end of January 1922, Narkomzem told him that he was being placed 'at the disposal of Comrade Krasin'.[19]   Krasin, as a member of the Soviet delegation, would be going to Genoa. Chayanov, however, would not go to Genoa. He, with his portfolio of preparatory documents, would be 'dispatched' to London, where Krasin's principal foreign trade office, 'Vneshtorg', was located.

In April 1922, Chayanov's personal life, and his professional life, had reached serious turning points. His first wife had left him for another man, an artist friend,[20] and Chayanov had just married for a second time. Now, he faced the fact that his effectiveness in the Commissariat had dwindled to a point where, as he would 'confess' later to Agranov, [*OGPU*, 10: 76] 'it became increasingly clear to me and to my colleagues in the Narkomzem that my role, necessary for the first year of the reconstruction period, was already at an end.'

To be sent on a business trip to Western Europe was almost as good as a vacation with all expenses paid, and a huge contrast to the fate of his friends, Prokopovich and Kuskova, who still languished in the provinces, condemned to internal exile, and soon to be banished from their homeland.

Kuskova had written to friends in Moscow that, although life was materially better in Kashin than in Vologda, thanks to gifts of food from friends, 'We live as in a prison, except that there is an exit to the street ... our moral condition is foul'. She wrote that 'every natural social intercourse with the outside world' was prohibited. At the same time, her husband, she said, was 'all work'. He had already sent two manuscsripts to the printer [*Russkoe Proshloe*, 4: 334–42].

The famine still gripped Russia. Three weeks before his scheduled departure for London, Chayanov took part in a public debate that was staged by the Third All-Russian Agrarian Congress, and pitted Agrarian-Marxists on one side against, as the newspaper *Pravda* put it, their 'detractors' on the other.

Pravda described the enormous crowd of would-be spectators, with and without tickets, who literally fought to get into the meeting hall, the prestigious House of Unions. The principal 'detractors' were Chayanov, Ber Brutskus and Nikolai Kondrat'ev. The main subject was the famine. The official Bolshevik position was that the famine had been caused by the ravages of the Civil War and by the damage done by the armies of foreign intervention.[21] Brutskus was most in tune with the interests of the crowd. He said bluntly that the government's agricultural policies were to blame for the famine. The Marxist reply came from Sergei Dubrovskii, who commented ('poetically', in *Pravda's* words) that Brutskus was sharpening arrows of private property aimed at the heart of the Soviet policy of land nationalisation. [*Pomoshch*: 3]. Chayanov had submitted 'Theses on Basic Agricultural Policy'[22] to the Congress, and he spoke at length in the debate about his vision of the future of agriculture in Russia. He was, it would seem, already writing, in his mind, his new book.

On 5 April 1922, both Krasin and Chayanov left Moscow. Krasin went as directly as he could to London, spent a day with his wife and children, who still lived there, partly because Krasin did not want to subject them to the privations of life at that time in Russia [*O'Connor*, 1992: 160–61], then travelled on to Genoa.

Chayanov stopped in Berlin long enough to meet briefly with Soviet representatives at a Tsentrosoyuz office, looked up members of the German academic community,[23] and at least one publisher, Alexander Yashchenko. Then, with his wife, he went on, by way of Paris, to England.

The Prague Archive has not provided dates, or locations, for many of the Chayanov letters that it has preserved. The first of the letters [Letters, 1], for example, is undated. It was directed to Prokopovich who, from the context, appeared to be still in Russia. Chayanov had settled, not in London, but in the countryside, where he was plunging into the preparation of his new book. The letter expressed the frustration of having to write, it would seem, mostly from memory.

As he put it: 'It is very hard to work without books.' His own books, and his notes and manuscripts, which he had packed in trunks and shipped to London from Moscow, had not yet arrived. His search for sources in England had been unproductive. He had found 'not a single book with an analysis of the social structure of the peasant farm with materials repeating the census material of Chernenkov, Kryashcheva, Vikhlyaev, Kushchenko and others'.

This complaint suggested that he was working on the first chapter of his book, which would deal with the development of the peasant family. Chernenkov and the others had gone back repeatedly, over periods of 10 to 30 years, to the same groups of farms to collect their census materials. Chayanov considered that, by so doing, their reports 'completely overthrew many of our conceptions about the peasant farm' and led to a new concept in statistical circles, that of 'Demographic Differentiation' in analyses of the dynamics of peasant farm size. He conceded that 'Social Differentiation' also was a factor, but asserted that it needed to be studied by other methods [*Chayanov*, 1966: 67–8]. In the 1920s, the matter of 'Social Differentiation' would become a highly-charged political question as the Bolsheviks began to classify peasants politically.

Chayanov wanted, as soon as possible, a copy of Prokopovich's new book on the derivation of correlation coefficients. This book would no doubt have been one of the works that Prokopovich had sent to the printer while he was in Kashin. He and Chayanov might well have discussed it before Chayanov's departure from Moscow. In this letter, Chayanov obviously believed that it was at least still possible that the Bolsheviks would permit the Prokopovich work to be printed in Moscow. In any case, without waiting to see the book, he wanted Prokopovich to send him right away the coefficients of correlation for families receiving only farming income compared with families receiving income from both farming and crafts and trades.

He was writing about the fact that peasant families traditionally turned to crafts and trades under certain conditions, and he wanted to determine 'what quantitatively determines the division of peasant labour between earnings from crafts and trades and earnings from agricultural work?' [*Chayanov*, 1966: 106].

Meanwhile, the Chayanovs enjoyed their little English village for its tranquillity, but were not impressed with its wine, food or weather.[24] Prokopovich's book was not published in Moscow.

On 1 June he and Kuskova passed through Moscow on their way out of the country [Letters, 2]. They were among the first to suffer a punishment that Lenin had ordered on 19 May, in his instruction to Secret Police Commissar Felix Dzerzhinsky: to begin preparations for 'the exile abroad of professors and writers helping the counter-revolution' [*Heller*, 1986: 142], a form of punishment that banished hundreds of Russia's most talented citizens.[25] Kuskova wrote to her friend, Vera Figner, on 1 June that she was leaving 'today' for abroad. 'Here in our homeland', she wrote, 'we have tried to survive the revolution, without success. Now, our task is otherwise – how not to become emigrants' [*Russkoe Proshloe*, 4: 339].

Like most of those who would follow, they went to Berlin. Maksim Gorkii, whom Kuskova had persuaded in 1921 to support the All-Russian Committee to Aid the Hungry, was already in Berlin. Lenin had ordered him to leave 'for the good of his health' in the autumn of 1921, while Kuskova and others were still in the Lubyanka prison. Gorkii welcomed Kuskova to Berlin at the end of June with a letter, saying, 'Your arrival is not surprising, since I knew already in April of the decision to banish all the members of the committee from Russia' [Letters, 3].

III

In England, Chayanov's devotion to his theoretical work on peasant farming had not kept him from worrying about less esoteric matters back home in Moscow. His most reliable link was his cousin, Sokrat Klepikov, to whom he wrote [Letters, 4] what he said rather petulantly was his third letter without an answer. He wanted information about a number of housekeeping matters, such as the 'Boyar's Palace', the elegant former mansion of Count G.A. Tsuyupov, built originally for the Boyar Volkov, where Chayanov wanted to (and later would) install his Institute of Agricultural Science and Policy in Moscow.[26] His unpleasant remarks about his brilliant colleague, Nikolai Kondrat'ev, probably reflected a worry that, while he was in England, Kondrat'ev might have been usurping his leadership of the Institute.

This letter identified his English residence as being in the town of Hildenborough, a hamlet in Kent 30 miles by rail from London.[27] A letter of 20 July to the Berlin publisher, Yashchenko, noted that he had received, at last, his trunks containing his books and scientific papers [Letters, 5]. He had sent Yashchenko 'a whole pile of agricultural literature' that had come in his trunks. Yashchenko's journal had already published, in Issue #5, one of Chayanov's articles, entitled: 'New Currents of Russian Economic Thinking', but Chayanov was most excited that Yashchenko was going to publish reviews of two of his romantic tales: *Venediktov* and *The Hairdresser's Mannequin*, as well as his very short and not very successful play, called *Obmanshchiki* (The Cheaters).

He knew by this time that Prokopovich and Kuskova were in Berlin, as this letter revealed when he referred to periodicals, such as *Agricultural Life*, and asked Yashchenko not to throw them on a shelf, or turn them over to Nikolaevski[28] when he was through with them, but 'to send them to the disposition of S.N. Prokopovich'.[29]

About the same time that Chayanov was retrieving his heavy baggage from Krasin's Vneshtorg office in London, Krasin was returning to his London home from an economic conference in The Hague.[30] Krasin stayed only a few days in London before travelling on to Moscow, but it would be reasonable to suppose that, while he was in London, he and Urquhart met and took the steps that revived the Urquhart concession agreement. It would be surprising if Chayanov, along with his portfolio containing material about concessions, was not called upon for these negotiations. Krasin and Urquhart would meet again in September, in Berlin, to sign the agreement.

Prokopovich and Kuskova had joined the extraordinarily vibrant emigrant community in what already was being called 'Russian Berlin' and the 'Third Capital of Russia'.

The Genoa Conference that Chayanov and Krasin had laboured to prepare, had been a failure, but the Russian–German treaty of Rapallo that it spawned had created a Moscow–Berlin axis favouring travel in both directions. Russian Berlin included the emigrants, like Kuskova and Prokopovich, who had been banished from Russia, as well as others who had left voluntarily and still others who had come to Berlin temporarily, just to taste the creative life of the place.

The vanguard of this Russian diaspora, coming mainly from Petrograd, had created a 'House of Arts' in Berlin.[31] It was a reincarnation of the facility in Petrograd that had been set up for the welfare of poets, writers, artists and musicians by Gorkii, with Lenin's blessing, soon after the revolution. The Berlin House of Arts welcomed Aleksei Tolstoi, Andrey Bely, Vladimir Mayakovskii, Boris Pasternak, Elza Triolet, Viktor Shklovskii, Ilya Ehrenburg, Vladimir Pozner, Boris Pilnyak, Marina Tsvetaeva, Aleksei Remizov, Evgenii Yesenin and his wife, Isadora Duncan, to name only a few [*Beyer*, 1987: 9–38].

None of the Russians in Russian Berlin considered themselves to be anything but Russians. Most of them, except for the unreconstructed Monarchists, considered themselves to be revolutionaries. Viktor Shklovskii [1970: 240] aptly described the revolutionary mind-set: 'During the first years of the revolution, there was no normal life in any sense, unless you consider a storm normal. There was not a man alive who did not experience periods of belief in the revolution. For whole minutes, you would believe in the Bolsheviks.'

Belief, or non-belief, in the Bolsheviks supplied the emotion in the political debates and disputes of Russian Berlin. The basic question was whether, or when, or under what conditions to go home. Those who had been expelled under the sweeping order of 1922, like Kuskova and Prokopovich, had been permitted to keep their passports, and the period of their banishment was theoretically three years. Most of them longed to go back, or, as Kuskova had put it, 'not to become emigrants'.

In June 1922, as Kuskova and Prokopovich arrived, Russian Berlin was consumed by two scandals: the 'show trial' of Socialist Revolutionaries (S-Rs) which had opened in Moscow on 8 June, and the announcement in Berlin by Count Aleksei Tolstoi that he would support the social-political movement called 'Changing Landmarks' and would write for its newspaper, *Nakanune* (On the Eve). The S-R trial was a scandal, at least partly, because Nikolai Bukharin had given delegates to a Congress of the Third International, in Berlin, a written promise that no death penalties would be sought. Lenin not only scolded Bukharin for making such a promise, he ordered Bukharin to participate in the prosecution. The death penalty was imposed. Gorkii, in what Lenin later called a 'filthy letter' to Anatole France, proposed a 'moral blockade' of the Soviet Union [*Fleishman*, 339–50].

Tolstoi's action was a scandal because it provided credibility to a highly controversial element in the émigré community. To change 'landmarks' meant to change the perception that the Bolsheviks were wild-eyed destroyers of Russia. Nikolai Ustrialov, a leading ideologist for 'Changing Landmarks', had summed up the philosophy in an article entitled 'The Radish', asserting that Russia was just that, 'a radish: red on the outside but white on the inside' [*Heller*, 1986: 145–51]. Lenin's New Economic Policy was viewed by the landmark-changers as proof that the Bolsheviks were changing. It followed, then, that émigrés should encourage the trend by 'changing their landmarks', joining the Bolsheviks in the quest for the strong, nationalist state that the Monarchy had failed to achieve.

After Tolstoi's move, the Berlin Union of (Russian) Journalists and Writers voted to exclude from its membership all collabourators with

Nakanune. 'Changing Landmarks' was something of a time bomb in Berlin's social-political cellar.

The month of June 1922 also saw the arrival of a delegation from Moscow to reopen the Russian embassy in Berlin. The city was immediately overrun with agents of the Secret Police, many of whom posed as members of the 'Changing Landmarks' movement.

Kuskova's plan to publish a newspaper in Berlin appeared in a letter that had arrived in Hildenborough in mid-August, and that Chayanov answered immediately [Letters, 6]. He bristled at her suggestion that he was carrying out a 'high communist assignment', but went on to applaud her intention to publish a 'genuine Russian newspaper'. When he spoke approvingly of the goal: 'to transform the russian problem from one of a struggle against the regime to one of redemption and re-birth of the homeland with all its enormous power …', he might seem, at first blush, to have echoed the 'Changing Landmarks' concept. However, he really was echoing Kuskova, who, in turn, with her background as a Konstitutional Democrat, appears to have been echoing the Cadet leader, Pavel Milyukov, one of the founders of the Cadet party. A year earlier, Milyukov had startled the emigrant community with a 'new tactic'. He had said to his fellow émigrés, 'I don't know whether you'll return to the homeland some day or whether you'll never return, but one thing I know – if you do return, it will never be on a white horse.' Kuskova's phraseology was less eloquent, but more to the point: '… let us fill in the trenches of the civil war' [*Osorgin*, 1982: 87].

Chayanov's point of view was that Kuskova's newspaper project would be a good one if she could run it 'as you would like to do it now, in today's Moscow, if there existed a free press'. His sarcasm about press freedom in Moscow extended to the emigré press in Berlin when he observed that they 'sing the *Internationale* upside-down'.

It was in this letter that he announced his task for the year: 'to create a scientific foundation for my basic social beliefs.' Something in Kuskova's letter prompted him to conclude his reply with the cryptic line:

'… The Utopia I banish, the pseudonym I seldom disclose!'

She must have referred to Yashchenko's Berlin journal, *Novaia Russkaia Kniga,* having published in its June issue, # 5, a notice saying: 'At the beginning of 1920 was published in Moscow under the pseudonym "Ivan Kremnev" the first part[32] of *Journey of my brother Aleksei to the Land of the Peasant Utopia.*'

The 'Utopia', and the 'pseudonym', were the burning subject of a second letter [Letters,7], sent on this same day, 13 August, appealing to

Yashchenko to handle the utopian fantasy with great circumspection. Chayanov tended to classify his Peasant Utopia, which was essentially a work of fiction, as one of his scientific, economic works. During interrogation by Secret Policeman Agranov, in 1930, he listed four works as his most significant writing on peasant theory in the period of 1917–22: *General Agronomics, Peasant Cooperation, Journey of my Brother Aleksei to the land of Peasant Utopia* (under the pseudonym I. Kremnev, published by Gosizdat) and the third edition of *Optimal Size of Agricultural Enterprises* [*OGPU*, 10: 66].

He had written the *Utopia* during the 'War Communism' period, before the NEP reforms, and his hero was living in that climate as the story opened, although Chayanov's narrative had given the date of the opening of his tale as October of 1921.

The hero, Aleksei Kremnev (fictitious brother of the fictitious author), had fallen asleep looking up at portraits of Thomas More, Edward Bellamy, Robert Blatchford and Charles Fourier:[33] 'In this fourth year of the revolution', Aleksei murmured to them, 'socialism may consider itself the undivided ruler of the globe. But you, pioneer utopists: are you satisfied?' Aleksei also wondered, as he dozed off: 'you, Milyukov and Novgorodtsev, Kuskova and Makarov, what kind of utopia might you design?' These four were real persons, not misty voices from the past. Kuskova and Makarov were Chayanov's close colleagues, in real life. The utopia about to be visited was a Kuskova–Makarov–Chayanov utopia.

When Brother Alexsei awakened, the year was 1984.[34] He had missed much history: 63 years to be precise. He had quickly learned (from a wise old man named Aleksei Minin, whose family had befriended him) that the communists had lost favour with the people back in the mid-1930s, that the peasants had slowly gained political as well as economic strength and now, in 1984, had become the majority party in a society where eveything ran on a co-operative basis.

Chayanov, in Hildenborough in the summer of 1922, was keenly aware that this vision of the future was far from what the Bolsheviks had in mind. Among the smaller heresies in his story was the description of a huge monument in central Moscow, in 1984, where the Hotel Metropole 'used to be'. Three heroic figures were featured in this utopian monument. Lenin was one. The other two were Kerenskii and Milyukov.

Little wonder that Chayanov did not want the pseudonym revealed, and did not want any reference to his 'prognostications of the course of history' – especially the defeat of communism in the 1930s. The mere mention of Ivan Kremnev has already 'cost me dearly. I do not wish to pour oil on the fire.'

On the other hand, publicity for his strictly literary pseudonym, 'Botanik X',[35] that he used for his romantic tales, was more than welcome. Chayanov's attention this summer was, in fact, somewhat less than totally focused on his seminal book about the peasant economy. He had not mentioned it just yet, but in spare moments, in Hildenborough, he had been writing another Hoffmanesque novelette, to be called *The Venetian Mirror, or the Remarkable Adventures of a Glass Person*.[36]

A fervent love of history was central to Chayanov's character. His romantic novels, and his '*Utopia*', were rich in scenes of Moscow life, and Moscow lore. His most serious interest, his agricultural research, had deep historical underpinnings, going back all the way to Ivan IV and Sylvester's household budgets (*Domostroi*).[37] Chayanov was an active member of the 'Old Moscow' Society. He was one of the founding fathers of the Museum of the History of Moscow. He was active in the Moscow chapter of the Russian 'Friends of Books' circle.

He had recreated detailed maps of the Moscow of 1737, of the Moscow of 1796, and of Moscow after the great fire of 1812. He had undertaken to catalog 'Moscow Collections of Paintings 100 Years Ago'. After the Bolshevik revolution, he had been a leader in efforts to save the pre-revolution treasures of Russia from mobs that sought to destroy everything old, a concern he shared with Krasin. During their brief stay in England, he and his wife spent time in research for a treatise and a small book that she was writing on the background of the Moscow theatre that had been, in fact, established by an Englishman named Maddox, and only later had come to be called the 'Bolshoi'.

With the approach of autumn and the 'fogs of Albion'[38] [Letters, 8], Chayanov's normal ebullience was deflated. Both he and his wife were ill. They were not sure whether Olga's problem was appendicitis or pregnancy, but the odds were that it was the latter. They were thinking of Berlin, at this point, because of its medical facilities. The last of Chayanov's books had arrived from Moscow, and he was getting a little work done, but still needed Prokopovich's correlation coefficients. His comment that publication of Prokopovich's book had been 'postponed' was a polite way of acknowledging that, as one who had been banished from his homeland, Prokopovich was now unlikely to have anything published in Moscow. Chayanov also referred to their exile when he inquired about the fate of several colleagues from the Committee to Aid the Hungry, including Kuskova's literary co-worker, Mikhail Osorgin, about whom Ol'ga was especially anxious.

Cousin Sokrat Klepikov[39] was a kindred spirit to Chayanov, as is seen in the next four letters, all addressed to him. Sokrat was thoroughly familiar with Chayanov's office on the Arbat (Nikolopeskovskii Lane) and would have no difficulty finding the Kushchenko books [Letters, 9]. Kushchenko was needed because Kushchenko's statistics covered a longer period of time than those of anyone else – 30 years – recording the ups and downs of the same farms, the same families, in the same part of Chernigov guberniya – Surazh. Chayanov was able, with Kushchenko's numbers, to demonstrate two 'powerful' currents. 'One, registered by the young, undivided farms with a small sown area, is rising, expanding the volume of its farms under pressure of family growth. The other is declining, largely due to the dividing of old, complex families' [*Chayanov*, 1966: 246–9].

The report that Arnol'd presented to the Third Congress of Naturalists and Physicians in 1901, one of the first experiments in the application of analytic geometry to the study of statistical variables in agricultural research, would be used in Chayanov's chapter on 'Basic Principles of Peasant Farm Organization', to illustrate the value of correlation analysis. Arnol'd's early work produced formulae that corresponded very closely to 'reality' [*Chayanov*, 1966: 103–4].

In other references to their agricultural interests, Chayanov recorded that he was writing his book on the peasant economy 'very assiduously and successfully'.

He had been to London and met with Zherebtsov, the agricultural agent at Krasin's Foreign Trade Mission, 'Vneshtorg', where he had made arrangements for sending things to and receiving things from Moscow. He noted that a copy of Olivet's *Historie Philosophique* that he was sending home cost 30 shillings – or 60 million Soviet Rubles. He identified his economist colleague and friend, Boris Knipovich, as his principal contact with Narkomzem while he was away [Letters, 9].

Although in Chayanov's letters, only Zherebtsov [Letters, 9], Braikevich and Buryshkin [Letters, 6], were mentioned as persons he saw in London, there were others that he certainly had seen, presumably including Krasin.

It is quite possible that he also saw Kuskova and Prokopovich. London was a principal source of funds for the kind of research institute that Prokopovich wanted to set up in Berlin. A 'Russian Academic Group' had already been established in Berlin to sponsor scholarly activities by Russian emigrés, and a Russian Institute was beginning to function. Chayanov, in his 12 August message [Letters, 6], seemed to be looking forward to a visit by Kuskova and Prokopovich, and a letter dated 10 September, from Prokopovich to Boris Bakhmetov, said that Prokopovich would be coming to London on the 13th and to Paris on the 21st [*Bakhmeteff*, Prokopovich Folder].

The plan to leave England at the end of October [Letters, 10] coincided with the prospect for a final decision on the Urquhart concession agreement. Krasin and Urquhart signed documents on the concession on 9 September. Lenin had decreed that it would be dealt with by a party plenum on 5 October [*Krassin*, 200]. The record shows that the Politburo debated the matter in meetings that Lenin did not attend, because of his ill health, on 14, 21 and 28 September and that the Plenum rejected the proposal on 6 October. There was only one 'yes' vote – Krasin's [*O'Connor*, 272].

So far as Chayanov's assignment to England may have related to the Urquhart affair, his presence would no longer have been required after the proposal's rejection. His reason for meeting with Osinskii in Berlin probably related to Krasin's vain hope to re-negotiate. Krasin and his delegation, in fact, were in Berlin late in October, but the Urquhart concession was a dead-letter. Krasin sent a notice of resignation, to which Lenin replied: 'We dismiss people from their posts, but we don't permit them to resign' [*Krassin*: 204].

The letters to Sokrat at the end of 1922 described in some detail the new passion of Chayanov and his wife for old engravings. By the time of their departure from England on 28 October [Letters, 10, 11] they had started a serious collection 'which included Rembrandt, Durer, Beham, Altdorfer and others'. They were very expensive at antique stores – 'one or two pounds apiece' – but cheap at junk dealers. Quite naturally, his thirst for antiquity had taken them to the British Museum, where Ol'ga sought information on the Maddox who built the Bolshoi theatre,[40] and where Chayanov learned to write his name, 'Alexandros', and Sokrat's name, 'Sokrates', in Egyptian hieroglyphics.

From Berlin, where they had planned to stay only briefly [Letters, 10] in a small boarding-house on Kleiststrasse, Chayanov was able to offer Sokrat a good deal of information about the city – where to stay if he received a visa and came for a visit, where to find the best places to shop for engravings, where to find friends and colleagues at the Berlin offices of Tsentrosoyuz and Narkomzem. Ol'ga was pregnant, and Chayanov hoped Sokrat would help them to find a nanny when they returned to Moscow [Letters, 12].

Krasin had gone to Italy for sunshine and rest. The Chayanovs were advised not to go to Italy, because of Ol'ga's delicate condition. They decided to prolong their stay in Berlin, or its environs. They were attracted to the resort area near the River Oder, amid the peaks of the Riesengebirge. First, however, there were social obligations to be be met.

They were invited to a gala banquet, arranged by the agricultural secretary of the Danish embassy, Andrei Koffod. [*OGPU*, 11: 99a]. Chayanov and Osinskii, and the representative of Narkomzem in Berlin, Fridrikhson, were the guests of honour. Two of Chayanov's academic acquaintances, specialists in Russian questions, Professor. Otto Auhagen and Professor Max Zering, were invited, as well. It would be Auhagen who would help Chayanov to publish his first article in Germany, in *Schmollers Jahrbuch*, and who would write a preface to his major work on the peasant economy, with its German title: *Die Lehre von der bäuerlichen Wirtschaft*. Chayanov considered Auhagen to be 'the godfather of my scientific activity in Germany' [*OGPU*,11].

Koffod was very attentive to the Russian visitors, invited Osinskii and Fridrikhson to join him on a tour of Denmark. Not too long afterward, Fridrikhson became Russia's trade representative in Denmark and Koffod became the agricultural attaché for the Danish Embassy in Moscow. Chayanov later credited Koffod with having a hand in finding a publisher for his book, the work that Dr Friedrich Schlömer would translate into German.

In 1930, the OGPU would build up a fanciful case around Koffod and his Russian assistant, Antonina Ushakova, charging them with being British spies. Koffod would be expelled from Russia. In 1937, Chayanov's friendship with Koffod would be the basis of the charge of treason and of his sentence to death [*OGPU*, 26: 449]. Ushakova would be executed in 1938. [*OGPU*, 26, 29].

At the end of 1922, Chayanov was cruising Berlin's several turbulent worlds. He introduced himself to German economists and agricultural scientists in Berlin and in other university centres. Zering invited him to participate in a major undertaking on the subject: 'The Status of World Agriculture and of Trade in Agricultural Products after the War.' Chayanov agreed to organize contributions from Russian scholars, including N.P. Makarov, N.P. Oganovskii, A.N. Chelintsev, B.N. Knipovich, G.A. Studenskii, N.D. Kondrat'ev, and others [*Balyazin*, 1990: 155].

Among the articles that Chayanov produced in this period was a 23-page work that undoubtedly reflected his recent stay in England. It was published in London in 1923, entitled 'The Current Status of the Linen Market and Possible Perspectives on the Sale of Russian Linen'.

He renewed his acquaintance with the publisher of *NRK*, Yashchenko, and met some of the many other editors and publishers who had created a huge and briefly prosperous printing world of their own. By this time, Mikhail Osorgin had arrived in Berlin. Kuskova introduced Chayanov to the sometimes violently active literary scene. The hostility stirred up by Alexei

Tolstoi's alignment with what many considered a pro-Bolshevik ideology continued to agitate the Russian literati.

Kuskova and Osorgin were, just at this time, organising a rival organisation to the 'House of Arts'. They called it the 'Writer's Club'. It was a reincarnation of the club of the same name in which Kuskova and Osorgin had been very active in Moscow, and its Moscow orientation was more than coincidental. The first wave of emigration had come to Berlin from Petrograd, the former capital of Russia, the birthplace of the revolution. It was natural for these émigrés to remember, and try to reproduce, the 'House of Arts' that they had known in Petrograd. Kuskova and Osorgin were of the second wave, coming mostly from the newly restored capital of Russia, Moscow. Their nostalgia was for their own Moscow 'Writer's Club', and their political orientation was different. Tolstoi would never be invited to the new club.

Also under way in Berlin was a very large and gaudy exposition of Russian artists, with Chagall, Kandinskii, Malevich, Rodchenko, Vasnetsov, Tatlin and scores of others represented. Chagall had used the occasion as an excuse to leave Russia. The Bolsheviks used it as a propaganda platform for the 'New Russia'.

Chayanov could scarcely have missed these aspects of life in Berlin, not only because of Kuskova's deep involvement in them, but also because both he and Ol'ga had been very much involved in literary, musical and artistic circles in Moscow.

They knew the Moscow artists. Chayanov chose very sophisticated illustrations for his romantic books. It was one of his illustrators, in fact, who had 'run off' with his first wife. His second wife, Ol'ga, was an authority on the Bolshoi Theatre. Russia's operatic prima donna, Antonina Nezhdanova, was a personal friend and would be a next-door neighbour in the co-op dacha community that Chayanov would start in Nikolina Gora, just outside of Moscow. The real life model for the hero of his story about the hairdresser's mannequin[41] was a prominent Moscow architect who built the mansion that would become the residence of the United States ambassador. Yet, nothing in the letters even hinted at an interest in Germany's great 'Bauhaus' movement, the spectacular examples of film and theatre, the modern art. Even in the area about which he did write to Sokrat, the art of engraving, he seemed to ignore Grosz , Schlichter, Bellmer and others, looking backward instead toward the old masters.

Among Berlin's attractions for Russians were its medical facilities. It was here that Russians who were really sick and could afford it always came for a cure. Gorkii was in a suburban sanitarium. Aleksei Rykov had undergone treatment in Berlin in 1921. Krasin had checked himself into a Berlin hospital after the failure of the Urquhart venture. It was a Berlin doctor who confirmed that Ol'ga Chayanova was pregnant.

IV

For Chayanov, Berlin, despite its importance as a cultural and scientific centre, was no place to live. As Christmas, 1922, approached, he and his wife stored many of their belongings with Kuskova and Prokopovich in Berlin and moved to the mountain village of Schreiberhau,[42] not far from the Czech border. There, he received from Prokopovich, by mail, a very important contribution to his book on the peasant economy, the long-awaited coefficients of correlation for the Vologda district.

He expressed his 'huge thanks', and promised to send the 'Vologda collection' back in two or three days – an indication that it may have been still in manuscript form. He described the snow that all but buried them, the visiting Makarov family, and the imminent arrival of his trunks full of books from London, then confessed to Prokopovich that he was having a little writing problem. He had found it necessary to rewrite the end of his chapter on Capital [Letters, 13].

This problem of clarity would still be a concern two years later, when he would sit down to revise his book for publication in Moscow, in Russian: he would actually consider entirely omitting the chapter on Capital, fearing that his concepts were so unusual that he might not find a common language with Russian readers. He would write that he had thought of trying to deal with the subject without using 'complex curves and conventional figures', but had realised that the fundamental subject of his analysis – 'the family farm's labour-consumer balance' – could not be expressed 'in any objectively final figures'. His solution would be to write several pages of explanation of his explanation, concluding with the proposition:

> At any particular level of technology and in a particular market situation, any labour family able to control the amount of land for use can increase its labour productivity by increasing the farm capital intensity to a certain level optimal for this family. Any forcing up of capital intensity beyond the optimum increases labour drudgery and even reduces its payment, since, on the one hand, increased expenditure to replace exhausted capital will counteract the useful effect of further capital intensification, while, on the other, the

economic realization of this capital requires the farm family to intensify its labour more than is permitted by the equilibrium of on-farm factors [*Chayanov*, 1966: 219–23].

With Prokopovich's Vologda information, Chayanov had no such problem. He would use it in several parts of his book, with full credit to Prokopovich, and then go on to write:

> The investigation of the peasant farm by correlation analysis of its elements is, unfortunately, in an embryonic state, despite a number of works already carried out. But, theoretically, we may foresee that we will have the following successive series of economic elements, the correlation coefficients of which will diminish as they become more distant from one another: the family (workers and consumers); personal consumption; total family output in farming, crafts, and trades; annual income from farming; harvest, sown area, and other technical elements of the farm (livestock, equipment, and so on).[43]

By Christmas, Chayanov's book, 'except for the introduction and the conclusion', would be finished, he wrote to Kuskova [Letters, 14]. He was in high spirits. They were living in 'such ideal conditions as can only be imagined'. The snow fell '26 hours a day'. Their guests, the Makarovs, had gone, but he and Nikolai Pavlovich had been able to solve all the world's problems for the next five centuries in the two days that the Makarovs had stayed. He could joke about the political spats in Berlin's émigré community, with a play on words using the names of the newspapers *Golos Rossii* (*Russia's Voice*) and *Dni* (*Days*), both of which were edited by prominent Socialist Revolutionaries, Viktor Chernov and Aleksandr Kerenskii, who loathed one another. There was reason to suppose that when, in October of 1922, *Dni* replaced *Golos Rossii*, and Kerenskii, in effect, replaced Chernov, the tone of the new 'gazette' would change. In the first 36 issues of Dni, however, Chayanov found that Kerenskii had 'matured' enough to 'restore and purify' the Socialist Revolutionary 'corpse'. He invited Kuskova to bring Prokopovich down to Schreiberhau for a jolly Christmas, with all the trimmings.

The 'Rhein' wine and Christmas cakes failed to lure Sergei Nikolaevich and Ekaterina Dmitrievna to Schreiberhau, but the prediction that his book would be practically finished by Christmas came to pass, and he could send to cousin Sokrat, along with his wishes for a Happy New Year, the news that he had signed: 'a contract with the publisher Paul Parey for publication in

German of my new book on the peasant economy and now I am making the final corrections in the already nearly finished text' [Letters, 15].

He also had found time for a trip to Cologne's bookstores and antique shops.

The Chayanovs' passports had been issued for one year, as of 31 January 1922, the date on which he had been formally assigned to go to London at Krasin's disposal. In his 'Happy New Year' letter to Prokopovich [Letters, 16], he noted that he would have to travel to Berlin by the end of January 1923, to renew their passports. Ol'ga's pregnancy would require them to stay on in Schreiberhau until March, when a short trip to Italy might be possible. They planned to return to Russia as soon as Ol'ga's health permitted, probably in October.

The return was very much on his mind, especially with respect to the offer to join the editorial staff of Prokopovich's new publication, *Ekonomicheskii Vestnik* (Economic Bulletin). Chayanov foresaw that, if he and Makarov were to be on Prokopovich's staff, they might have problems with 'the ordinary Chekist'[44] when it came to returning to Moscow. Apparently, his old colleague, Brutskus, had been invited to join the new publication, and would, Chayanov suggested, represent their views quite well. Brutskus, unlike Chayanov and Makarov, had definitely emigrated from Russia and had no need to care what the Secret Police thought. The 'co-operative days' that Chayanov rather haughtily disdained to attend may have been part of a Soviet propaganda campaign that was being carried on in Germany by Willi Muenzenberg's Communist Youth International, headquartered in Berlin [*Willett, 1978*: 71]. Chayanov was eager, on the other hand, to take part in a seminar at the 'institute',[45] as he polished off his book prior to its publication. He would use the same pedagogic techniques that he and Prokopovich had developed at the Shanyavskii University. In this letter, Chayanov, after buttering up Prokopovich with lavish praise of his 'pioneer' work in the development of Russian economic thought, blithely proceeded to challenge aspects of Prokopovich's most recent work. He found 'insuffcent elaboration' in some parts. He thought that what Prokopovich had written about the 'receipt of profit' did not offer much on a theoretical level. He thought it was rather a waste of time to compare income with the sowing area of farms since all such elements described the same thing, the size of agricultural activity.

His objection in terms of 'specific gravity' touched on a concept that Chayanov took very seriously. 'Specific gravity', he wrote, was missing from the Prokopovich 'coefficients of land values'. What were needed were comparisons, not of a family's income from agriculture, but of the family's general income, and, what was most important, the income of a single worker. Chayanov was elaborating this point of view in his Chapter One of the *Peasant Family:*

> In studying the road along which the peasant farm develops, we ought to notice that to convert the number of family working hands into farm size and income we must additionally determine: to what extent these hands may be utilized; what part of potential working time is actually expended; what is the intensity of their labour or its degree of self-exploitation; what are the available technical means of production with which labour enters the production process; how high, in the final result, will be the productivity of this labour, depending on natural conditions and the market situation. Only when we have compared the pressure of family size with the influence of these factors, establishing their interrelationships and the specific gravity of each one in determining the structure and volume of the peasant family's economic activity, can we also approach a knowledge of the nature of the peasant farm [*Chayanov,* 1966: 69].

During a trip to Berlin, he had talked to Makarov, who had been scheduled to be there 13–15 January. He had been 'terrified' to learn [Letters, 17] that Makarov had, to some degree, unmasked him as the author of the *Peasant Utopia.* The Hall of Columns in Moscow had already been established, with the trial of Socialist Revolutionaries in June of 1922, as a location for 'show trials' where anyone who deviated from the official line could be publicly disgraced and dealt with as a criminal. Chayanov had no wish to be caught up in 'all that publicity-political bravado'.

He had reason to be fearful. His arrest, in 1930, would be part of a grandiose plan to stage three interconnected show-trials in the same Hall of Columns: a trial of the mythical 'Toiling Peasants Party', of which he and his associates – Makarov and Kondrat'ev among others – were supposedly the leaders, a trial of a mythical 'Industrial Party', and a third trial involving a group of so-called Menshevik counter-revolutionary conspirators. The second and third trials would, in fact, take place, but Chayanov and his group would be convicted in secret sessions of the military court, and Chayanov's *Peasant Utopia* would be instrumental in his downfall.

Rashit Yangirov [1989: 161–2], in his study of Chayanov's semi-utopian film about agriculture, *Albidum, or Victory over the Sun* , noted that OGPU interrogator Agranov had no real evidence against Chayanov, but 'found everything he needed' for his interrogation in the journey of brother Alexei.

Chayanov's five letters to his cousin Sokrat, from mid-January to mid-March [Letters, 18–22] dealt with three principal subjects: his various writing projects, his joint work with Sokrat on the collection of engravings, problems with his ex-wife in Moscow. Not surprisingly, he wrote not a word about his fear of a backlash from his peasant utopia. That was not something he would want to mention in letters going to Moscow.

He did express to Sokrat his concern about possible problems if there were 'too great a noise' about his and his ex-wife's housing difficulties. Muscovites, at this moment, were living through the period so tellingly described by Mikhail Bulgakov in *Heart of a Dog*, in which draconian restrictions were being placed on the number of square metres a tenant might legally occupy, with citizens' committees joyfully cracking down on anyone who might be considered bourgeois. He wanted his ex-wife to continue to live, legally, in the house that they had occupied together, on Degtyarnii Lane. He and his new wife, with the new child they were expecting, hoped to move into pleasant quarters at the Agricultural Academy when they returned. He also admitted to his mixed feelings, that 'Our life's path, Elena Vasilievna's[46] and mine, is finished forever, but I can not tolerate having a person who shared my life for nine years to experience need at a time when I am in a position to help her.' He wanted to help, but he did not want her to know that he was helping, and he was distressed to learn that she had been told that he had sent her a bountiful Christmas present.

Cousin Sokrat had been struggling with a mysterious illness, and had even consulted a 'witch doctor'.[47] Sokrat also wanted desperately to visit Germany on his own, and Chayanov had been pulling strings to help, one string being Osinskii, who had been 'living here for three months'. Osinskii's arrival in Berlin in October of 1922, and Krasin's, had coincided with Chayanov's departure from England and arrival in Germany. When the Urquhart concession had failed to materialise, and Krasin had gone off to Italy to pout in the sun, then back to London, Osinskii and the delegation had remained in Berlin. Even as Chayanov wrote about Osinskii to cousin Sokrat, however, Krasin was on his way to Berlin to rejoin Osinskii and the delegation and return with them to Moscow in mid-February [*O'Connor*, 1992: 274]. Chayanov would see them before their departure.[48]

Chayanov was publishing his 'fat' book[49] in the German language and had already had two articles accepted for publication.[50] He thought he would be coming home in the autumn with three books, not one, plus something about 'Old Engravings'.

His address after 3 March would be in Heidelberg, and on 2 March he

wrote 'my last letter from Schreiberhau. Tomorrow morning we leave for
Heidelberg and expect to be there until our return to Moscow.' Apparently,
he and Ol'ga had given up their plan to visit Italy.

V

A few days before they said good-bye to Schreiberhau, Chayanov had
learned that the literary editor of Kerenskii's newspaper, *Dni*, Alexander
Baxrax, had published a critique of his fanciful tale, *Venediktov*. Kuskova
had suggested that Baxrax, who was the secretary of her 'Writer's Club' in
Berlin, might be interested in the 'literary experiment' of a prominent
economist who wrote fiction under a pseudonym, 'Botanik X'. Baxrax later
recalled [1982] that, when he had read the novelette, he had decided that this
Botanik X was worth noticing, that it was 'time to write about him'.

Chayanov was thrilled to be 'noticed' as Botanik X, and the two men
struck up a warm friendship. Baxrax called Chayanov his 'buddy',[51] and
Chayanov called Baxrax his 'namesake'.[52] They had the same name and
patronymic: 'Alexander Vasilievich.' In mid-March, they met in Berlin, at
which time Chayanov expressed his gratitude to Baxrax by autographing
two of his publications: *Obmanshchiki* and *Istoriya Parikmaxerskoi Kukly*
(*The Affair of the Hairdresser's Mannequin*) [Letters, 23, 24]. Chayanov
discussed his belletrist activities with Baxrax, especially his newest tale,
The Venetian Mirror, which he had drafted in London and now was trying
to re-write. He hoped Baxrax might help him to have it published in Berlin.

At just this time a small army of German doctors was being dispatched
from Berlin to Moscow to deal with Russia's number one invalid, Lenin,
who had suffered a massive stroke on 9 March. Although he would survive
as a 'living corpse' for another nine months, there was a leadership crisis in
Moscow. Russians, at home and abroad, while they might have known little
of the true nature of Lenin's brain damage, were beginning to sense the
confusion at the summit of power.

From Heidelberg, Chayanov admitted to Kuskova [Letters, 25] his own
sense of insecurity, the 'helpless' feeling of the expectant father. He noted
that his mother was grateful for Kuskova's assistance in bringing her to
Germany where she would be available to help with the approaching birth
of his and Ol'ga's child. He and Ol'ga were, he said, becoming, in all
aspects, 'dwellers of Heidelberg'.

One of the advantages for Chayanov of being a Heidelberg dweller was
his access to the University and its resources, both human and archival. The

sociologist-economist Professor Alfred Weber, whose work on the theory of 'Standort' appealed to Chayanov, was a fixture on the faculty of the University. Weber's theory dealt with the location of industrial enterprises, and Chayanov saw it as a model for the development of a Russian-oriented theory of location in agriculture. It also was very useful to Chayanov that there was, in Heidelberg, the editorial office of the German scientific journal, *Archiv fur Sozialökonomie und Sozialwirtschaft,* although the journal was actually printed in Tübingen. On 18 April, Chayanov mentioned in a letter to Prokopovich [Letters, 26] that he was 'in close contact' with the journal's Heidelberg personnel. He disclosed that: 'The other day, I finished *To the Question of Economic Theory of Non-Capitalist Systems of National Economies*'[53] which would be printed, he said, in the *Archiv.* This theoretical essay would exacerbate a certain estrangement in his professional, although not his personal, relationship with Prokopovich, a trend that may have started with his earlier polite, but firm, rejection of the scientific value of some of Prokopovich's budgetary work [Letters, 16].

One reason for the elaborate apology concerning the missing Chernenkov books [Letters, 26] was that Chernenkov was one of the prime sources of information on which Chayanov's theory of 'demographic differentiation' was based, a position that Prokopovich challenged. In this connection, Chayanov mentioned similar studies made in Tula province, in Epifansk district, by Anna Khryashcheva, who also, he pointed out, had written similarly about the Moscow region.

The weeks of spring and early summer, as Ol'ga's pregnancy approached term, found Chayanov working on not just one, but two projects of fiction, his *Venetian Mirror* and a new, much more ambitious work that was still no more than an idea.

In mid-April, he wrote to Baxrax [Letters, 27] enclosing the 'final version' of *Mirror.* He asked Baxrax to represent him in a discussion with Abram Vishniak[54] about publishing the book, and spelled out his requirements.

His demand for the 'new orthography' was a quasi-political, as well as an aesthetic, statement. The modernisation of the cyrillic alphabet had been completed in Russia before the war, but its application had been postponed. Thus, it had fallen to the Bolsheviks to put it into effect, and anti-Bolshevik émigré writers were emotionally divided on the subject. Many insisted on having their works published in the old, traditional alphabet.

On or about the second of May 1923, Chayanov sent his brief letter to cousin Sokrat [Letters, 28] along with a colour-print from a wood engraving carved by himself, announcing the birth of his son, Nikita.

A few days later, there was good news from Baxrax. *Mirror*, it seemed, would be published, although at Chayanov's expense. He replied immediately [Letters, 29], with deep thanks and some questions about transferring money (an amount Baxrax later indicated was 11 British pounds). The problem was Germany's rampant currency inflation. It was now three months since French and Belgian troops had reoccupied the Ruhr, an action that had triggered a widespread wave of 'passive resistance', with a nearly complete stoppage of economic activity in Germany's most important industrial region. The government in Berlin had begun printing money as fast as the presses could turn it out.

On the one hand, this made life, for foreigners, extremely cheap. On the other hand, exchanging hard currency became an adventure. German merchants began to introduce their own 'coefficients of correlation'. Instead of constantly printing new prices on their wares, merchants were substituting a money market coefficient that varied along with the rates of exchange. The nominal price of the newspaper *Rul'* remained at 1 Mark. Applying the coefficient of the day, or the hour, *Rul'* would cost 400 Marks on 1 June, 1,000 Marks on 1 July and 150,000 Marks in September. The magnetism of Berlin and Germany that had attracted Russians was changing polarity. Communists were forming 'Red Hundred' militia groups, planning a Communist revolution on the anniversary, 7 November, of the Bolshevik takeover in Russia. In Munich, beer hall politics foreshadowed Fascism. *Rul'*, on 27 May, published a large article headlined: 'Arguments about Emigration', dealing with the question of 'going home'. Many were beginning to do just that.

Russian émigrés who, in 1921 and 1922, had embroiled themselves in passionate but relatively good-natured disputes, now declined even to speak to or associate with one another. Chayanov's and Kuskova's friend, Osorgin, had refused to allow his work to be published in journals that printed material from two of his critics, Zinaida Gippius and Vladislav Khodasevich [*Osorgin*, 1982: 93].

Chayanov's 8th of May letter to Baxrax [Letters, 30] revealed a rare attack of self-doubt. He had re-written *Mirror* so many times he could not stand the thought of working on it any longer. Still, if Baxrax thought it worth publishing, he was ready to go ahead, get some art work done and get it out of the way – all, he hoped, in a month or less.

On the fringes of Chayanov's life, disquieting things were happening, some knowledge of which certainly must have been available to him from his Narkomzem and Tsentrosoyuz contacts in Berlin.

Lenin's virtual disappearance from the scene was one. The 12th Party

Congress had been held without him. Krasin's position was weakening. Chayanov surely had at least heard rumours that Krasin was being replaced as plenipotentiary in London. And then there was the the event of 10 May, the assassination at an international conference in Lausanne of the man who was supposed to replace Krasin in London, V.V. Vorovskii, the same Vorovskii who had been been in charge of the publication of, and had written the preface to, Chayanov's *Peasant Utopia*.

What we know from his letters is that all his free time, now, away from his scientific work, was focussed on a new 'big' novel, about a certain Count Buturlin. On 22 May, he advised Baxrax [Letters, 31]: '... *Buturlin* is all written and I am mailing you a fair copy'. A few days later [Letters, 32], he announced that he would be arriving in Berlin on June 10 and wanted to read the Buturlin novel to Baxrax. Reading aloud was standard practice for Russian writers. Chayanov was well known for his voice and his dramatic presence. Students always flocked to his seminars just to hear him. At home, when there were guests, he would usually provide the entertainment by reading something he had written. In this case, the only person other than Baxrax whom he particularly wanted to hear him was Mikhail Osorgin's wife, Rakhila.

One of several letters from Heidelberg to Narkomzem in mid-June has been preserved in the TsGANX archive in Moscow, disclosing that Chayanov had not neglected his government assignment, and had been busily buying books. [Letters, 33]. His letter to Gennadi Studenskii [Letters, 34] portrayed Chayanov the taskmaster, prodding the scholars who were working, at his direction, on Professor Zering's ambitious book about world agricultural trade.

Berlin's social, literary and political life was closing down for the summer. Yashchenko's journal, *Novaia Russkaia Kniga*, had announced its summer recess. This summer would hear, in fact, the swan song of Russian Berlin. The prosperity of the émigré publishers was a thing of the past. Bankruptcies were the talk of the town. The inflation had ruined everyone.

The *NRK* would never re-open. It was out of business.

Earlier in the year, Yashchenko had lamented the concomitant deterioration in Berlin's émigré political life. Their society, he wrote, needed to be composed 'not of Communist, nor of Smenovektsi, nor of Monarchist, nor of Wrangltsi, nor of Cadet, nor of Eser of Chernovskii doctrine, nor of Eser of Kerenskii doctrine'.[55] They all needed, he said, to be 'au dessus de la mêlée'.

Kuskova was caught up in this mêlée, categorised as a 'fellow traveller' with the 'Changing Landmarks' movement as well as with the 'Eurasians'.

Donald Fiene has described it more objectively [*Osorgin*, 1982: 83], 'the question in the summer of 1923, was about "going home"', and there were three major factions dealing with it. First was the 'Changing Landmarks' group that advocated an 'about face' in their former critical attitude toward the Bolsheviks. Second was the 'Eurasian' group, advocating an 'Exodus to the East'. Third were people associated with E.D. (Ekaterina Dmitrievna)'.

A leader in the vilification of Kuskova was Alexander Yablonovskii, a polemicist writing for the newspaper *Rul'*, a fierce opponent of all who appeared to be 'soft' on Bolshevism. (He would later join Milyukov in Paris, and become vice president of the Paris Union of Russian Writers and Journalists.)

Chayanov told Kuskova [Letters, 36]: 'you are not to blame that Messrs. Yablonovskii in their time could not get passing grades in even a preparatory class in political literacy', and he applauded her 'civil courage', but he suggested that her efforts to reason with her opponents would bring, at best, a Pyhrric victory.

He continued to insist that Kuskova and her husband come to taste the delights of Heidelberg, but he was resigned to the fact that it would not occur, and his dear friends would not give the Chayanovs the chance to show off their son, Nikita.

He politely asked Prokopovich once more [Letters, 35] to come for a visit, but the general tone of Chayanov's correspondence with Prokopovich was changing. In this letter, responding to criticism of his book by Prokopovich, he admitted that he had been aware for some time of Prokopovich's 'discontent' with him, 'which finally appears in full light'. He defended his formulation of the labour-consumption balance by declaring that he was in full compliance with the work of Gessen and Jevons, who long ago had discerned something similar to his labour-consumption balance. If there was a complaint about his use of correlations, Chayanov said, it was the fault of Prokopovich 'since you still have not published the full results of your research'.

He concluded with a friendly request for 'instructions' concerning the scientific work he intended to do when he would be back at home in Moscow, and he signed the letter with his usual 'A.Ch.'. Curiously, this letter was written on stationery with the formal letterhead of Chayanov's institute in Moscow, and after the 'A.Ch.', he had added, in parentheses '(Professor A.V. Chayanov)', almost as though he felt a need to remind Prokopovich of his academic credentials.

The chill in relations with Prokopovich persisted. On 10 August [Letters, 37] he was 'very sad' to have received a letter 'in such a critical and cold form'. His old friend had hit him with a series of criticisms of both *Theory of Peasant Economy* and his recent article on economic theory in non-capitalist systems. He apparently had criticised Chayanov for identifying communism as a qualified economic system, for espousing 'Eurasianism', and for incorrectly employing a 'fixed growth of consumption' in his labour-farm theory.

The complaint about communism related to a table in Chayanov's treatment of non-capitalist economies, in which he outlined eight 'economic categories': Capitalism, Commodity Economy, Natural Economy, Slave Economy, Quitrent Serf Economy, Landlord Economy, Peasant Economy, Communism – in other words, Capitalism and seven non-Capitalist systems, all seven of which defied, in his view, analysis with Capitalist formulae. Chayanov agreed with Prokopovich that Communism 'negates economy' in the sense of 'empirically customary economics', but he pointed out that he had devoted an 'insignificant' space to it in his essay, and he defended its inclusion in his table as a 'conceivable system'. It would be more helpful of Prokopovich, he said, to comment on his concepts of 'slave and serf economies'.

The charge of 'Eurasianism' he dismissed out of hand, chiding Prokopovich for founding his criticism on 'assumptions' drawn from political conclusions about the Chayanov theory of the labour-farm. This was a dispute that had dogged Chayanov and Prokopovich for a long time, based on Prokopovich's firm adherence to Marxist analysis and Chayanov's rejection of the scientific viability of such analysis for the family farm without hired labour.

He did not come out and say it, in this letter, but it was clear that Chayanov felt that Prokopovich was simply throwing the 'Eurasian' label at him because it was a convenient imprecation of the moment: Chayanov rejected a Western concept, therefore Chayanov was embracing the Eurasian theory. Chayanov here, as in many of his works, made it quite clear that the unique elements of the peasant farm were not, in his view, geographical, or racial, or historical or religious. They were just inevitable organisational elements of such a farm anywhere. In the second paragraph of his theory of non-capitalist systems, he emphasised that 'most peasant farms, in Russia, China, India – in most non-European and even in many European states – are unacquainted with the categories of wage labour and wages' [1966a: 7].

Chayanov bristled at the Prokopovich reference to Litoshenko, a long-time colleague, who had become a strident critic of the 'drudgery' concept. When he updated his book on the peasant economy for publication in

Russia, Chayanov dealt in the introduction with his and Litoshenko's basic argument [1966: 47]:

> It is true that L.N. Litoshenko doubts that the psychology of the labour consumer balance is characteristic of this sector, and insistently suggests avarice as the basic feature of peasant psychology. In this instance, however, it is necessary to agree on precisely what is the psychology of avarice and what is the labour-consumer balance. Of course, our critics are free to understand the labour-consumer balance theory as a sweet little picture of the Russian peasantry in the likeness of the moral French peasants, satisfied with everything and living like the birds of the air. We ourselves do not have such a conception, and are inclined to believe that no peasant would refuse either good roast beef, or a gramophone, or even a block of Shell Oil Company shares, if the chance occurred. Unfortunately, such chances do not present themselves in large numbers, and the peasant family wins every kopek by hard, intensive toil. And in these circumstances, they are obliged not only to do without shares and gramophones, but sometimes without the beef as well.
>
> It seems to us that if Rothschild were to flee to some agrarian country, given a social revolution in Europe, and be obliged to engage in peasant labour, he would obey the rules of conduct established by the Organization and Production School, for all his bourgeois acquisitive psychology.

The other criticisms by Prokopovich were dismissed in Chayanov's letter as just further instances of his being blamed for 'childish' mistakes that he, himself, had long ago recognised, and had long ago corrected. In this case, it was the 'variability of the growth of consumption'. All criticisms of his work would be discussed and disposed of, he predicted, in a 'new Russian edition of his Principles of a Peasant Economy'.

His confidence that all disagreements would be easily removed in one evening of face-to-face discussion 'if you admit the necessity of recognizing a theory of peasant farming without the idea of wages and the simple profit of Capitalist thought' reflected Chayanov's supreme confidence in his ability to win any debate.

Regarding Eurasianism, Chayanov felt that, even here, they could find several points of agreement, if Prokopovich would 'exclude problems of the present day, in relation to which we conceive even the facts differently'.

Before this letter could be delivered in Berlin, the German government had lost a vote of confidence. A new chancellor, Gustav Stresemann, had assumed power. He would launch a successful program of monetary stabilisation, one result of which would be a huge increase in the cost of living, far beyond the means of most Russian émigrés.

Chayanov searched his soul in the next letter. As preserved in the Prague archive [Letters, 38], it had no date, no salutation. Written at about the time of the ratification in Moscow of a Constitution for the new Soviet Union, in the midst of the emigré turmoil over antagonistic views about 'going home', and as the day of his own scheduled return to Moscow drew nearer, it presented to Kuskova the pros and cons of return.

One may suppose that the letter began, in the portion that is missing, with consideration of what would be involved in not returning, a course of action that would somehow involve the 'West, and a place in a cemetery'.

A decision to return, it seemed clear to Chayanov, meant that the intelligentsia must examine Soviet economic programs with 'objectivity', identify 'obstacles' to progress that the Soviet regime was creating, and deal with them however, and whenever, that became possible.

His 'fantastic' vision for spurring Russian recovery based on the sale of economic concessions to Western industries revealed how closely he had followed the saga of the Urquhart affair, and how thoroughly he had absorbed the policies of Krasin, not only the ideas, but the very words. Chayanov was 'in favour of intervention, not military, but economic.' Krasin had 'described Urquhart as the "essence of the spirit of European intervention" against Soviet Russia' [O'Connor, 1992: 273] Krasin had considered that, 'having resolved to invest in the Soviet state, Urquhart's decision essentially meant the "elimination of military intervention"'.

It was, for Chayanov, a matter of 'either-or': he could decide either *to go* – because 'the power is there, not here'; or *not to go*: – 'if there is no vista ...'.

The decision to return to Moscow had been made by 21 August 1923, when he wrote to his old friend in Switzerland [Letters, 39], Professor Ernst Laur, whom he had first met during a youthful trip to Western Europe in 1912. He was delighted that he could complete the circle of his book, conceived and begun under the aegis of Laur, in 1912, and now, with his thanks for Laur's help and inspiration, concluded.

Prokopovich, apparently, had been downright insulting [Letters, 40] in his reaction to the final version of *Die Lehre von der bäuerlichen Wirtschaft*, which Dr Friedrich Schlömer had translated into German. Schlömer had turned the Russian manuscript over to Prokopovich. Chayanov noted that, in Chapter 3 of his new book, he 'took into consideration your criticism and your oral remarks ...'. At the same time, he struck back with the comment that, in order to seriously criticise his book, it behooved Prokopovich to come up with a real theory, which his works on correlation coefficients, for all their value, had not produced. He challenged Prokopovich to a kind of duel: 'theory against theory'.

Years later, Basile Kerblay noted that Prokopovich's book, published in Berlin in 1924 as an open challenge to Chayanov's book, had not met the criterion for challenge. Kerblay found Prokopovich's book 'disappointing, since it did not live up to its claims. It was not, in fact, a new theory of peasant economy but a collection of more or less connected essays on different aspects of this economy before the Revolution' [*Chayanov*, 1966: lxvii].

Chayanov undoubtedly met at least once more with Prokopovich, if only to collect the Russian manuscript of his book, his one and only complete text [Letters, 40]. He was concerned about a speech Prokopovich had delivered in Prague, presumably at a conference of academic organisations in the diaspora, arranged by the Russian Academic Group in Berlin [*Raeff*, 1990: 82]. He cautioned Prokopovich not to break his ties to Russian agrarian circles, and, indeed, Prokopovich would continue for a number of years to write about the Soviet economy, from Prague and from Switzerland.

The newspaper *Rul'* announced in September that, with the cessation in Berlin of Russian theatre activity, most of the Russian artists had relocated abroad, mostly in Paris. A liquidation sale was organised for one of the main publishing houses, Grzhebin. In October, *Rul'*, now selling for 80 million Marks per copy, announced that: 'On Saturday, October 20, the Writer's Club is closing in view of the departure from Berlin of a considerable majority of the organisation's members. It is possible that the activity of the Club, which originated in Moscow and was later transferred to Berlin, will be revived in Paris.'

Alexei Remizov and Vladislav Khodasevich left for Paris. Maksim Gorkii went to Sorrento. Marina Tsvetaeva went to Prague. So did Prokopovich and Kuskova. Aleksei Tolstoi and Andrei Bely returned to Russia. So did Chayanov.

A glimpse of the reality that Chayanov faced on his return to Russia emerges from a letter that he wrote to Kuskova and Prokopovich from Paris [Letters, 41] in 1927. He had been permitted to leave on another, much shorter trip to Western Europe, and was staying, with his wife, in a fine hotel just a block from the Élysée Palace.[56]

Despite the fact that it was their early work on co-operatives that had attracted Chayanov and Prokopovich to one another, he made no mention of the publication in Moscow of his book on the theory of peasant cooperatives, a recent, and major work. The letter tried to be cheerful, and revealed that he still had very warm feelings for Prokopovich, despite their differences over economic theory, but his discussion of life in Moscow had a stiff-upper-lip quality, a tone that sounded as though he was well aware of pitfalls that awaited him at home.

VI

In the summer of 1930, when he had ended up in a cell in Lubyanka, just as he had told Yashchenko he feared might happen, he reviewed for his Secret Police interrogator, Agranov, his year and a half stay abroad [*OGPU*, 11: 97–102]:

> In 1922, at the time of my stay in Germany, I published in two fundamental economic journals, *Schmolers Jahrbuch* and *Archiv für Sozialökonomie und Sozialwirtschaft*, articles about the situation of the agricultural economy in the U.S.S.R., in which I set forth, for the most part, the work of the Neonarodnik group (Chelintsev, Makarov, Rybnikov and myself).
>
> With these articles, my name became more or less known by the scientific circles of Germany, and they gave me the possibility, the following year, to publish in the press of Paul Parey my basic book, *Die Lehre von der bäurlichen Wirtschaft*, which was very well received by the press and by scientific circles. Originally, I intended to publish the book under the aegis of the Institut,[57] but N.N. Krestinski[58] considered that to be improper and it came out with only my dedication to the Institute.

Chayanov described a world-wide directory of agricultural scientists that he compiled, and that he called Minerva, to serve as a correspondence network. His first circular letter, he said, drew around 70 responses. He told Agranov:

> The next year (1924), to many of these addresses, I sent my second German book, *Socialagronomie*, and for that purpose divided the network of correspondents into three categories of importance. I began to rely on the Institute's apparatus to send each year three or four of the books produced by the Institute, receiving books and letters in exchange.

This systematic work produced a network of correspondents in 60 locations, as well as around 120 circulating correspondents, embracing Germany, Denmark, Holland, Norway, Poland, Lithuania, England, Estonia, France, Italy, Austria, Czechoslovakia, Switzerland, Greece, Syria, Turkey, India, Siam, Australia, New Zealand, China, Japan, Honolulu, Canada, the U.S.A., Mexico, Uruguay, Honduras, Argentina, South Africa. Thanks to these connections, I succeeded in all these countries in creating an esteem for Soviet science, and in receiving a more or less clear representation of their scientific work.

The creation of this network, in Chayanov's opinion, was quite helpful to Soviet affairs. He feared, however, that because of 'the disintegration of these contacts, which began after I, personally, discontinued this work, it [the network] has been thoroughly destroyed'.

Not only was Chayanov's network destroyed; his published works, his theories, his name, almost all record that he had ever even existed were buried. As A.A. Nikonov[59] put it, 'his scientific activities were broken with the arrest of June 1930[60] ... the name of A.V. Chayanov, until recent times, was unknown by our contemporaries. Two generations were deprived of his scientific legacy'.

Viktor Danilov, possibly the most astute observer of Chayanov's life and work, suggests that this act of obliteration was not necessarily mere mindless Bolshevik terror. In his introduction to a re-issue of the *Theory of Peasant Co-operatives* [1991b], Danilov puts it this way:

The idea of 'co-operative collectivization' reflected the basic tendency of the actual development of co-operation in the Russian countryside in the 1920's, and offered a real alternative to collectivization of the Stalinist variety. This was quite enough to ensure that the book would very soon be condemned and banned; and that its author would be among the first victims of Stalinist repression.

Chayanov had the ambition, when he went to Europe in 1922, to establish a scientific basis for his social beliefs. When he debated whether to go back to Russia in 1923, in his last letter from Heidelberg to Kuskova [Letters, 38], it was clear to him that, because the power was *there*, his place was *there* – if he could hope to have an impact on the growth of the national economy, if he could, with objectivity, 'reveal ever more clearly the obstacles, created by the Soviet regime, to the development of the national economy'.

He was willing to try. When the order was issued for his arrest, the OGPU agents found him in his office in the 'Boyar's Palace', hard at work on a status report for his then chief employer, Zernotrest, the Soviet super-agency established by Stalin to create and run giant state farms [*Stalin Report*, 1930: 62–8].

As for those 'social beliefs' that needed a scientific foundation, perhaps he best stated them in his *Peasant Utopia* through the character of Aleksei Minin: 'In the construction of Peasant Russia we must develop – not freedom of government, so much as – freedom from government.'

NOTES

1. *Die Lehre von der Baüerlichen Wirtschaft ...* (*The Theory of Peasant Economy*).
2. When his prosecutors decided that he was guilty of counter-revolutionary activity, Chayanov was transferred from the Inner Prison of Lubyanka to the Butyrki prison in Moscow. From there, on 4 June 1931, he wrote a letter to the Secret Political Department of OGPU, describing five projects on which he had been working in prison, and adding: 'Besides these, in my briefcases (obviously among the papers taken during the perquisition) there were some dozens of others of my important works and a huge number of rough drafts, notes, materials collected over 20 years of scientific work, literally from the entire world, extracts of whole libraries, unique data never before published, and other papers.' He asked that all this be saved. None of it has come to light.
3. The interrogation material was made available to this writer, with the help of Vasilii Aleksandrovich Chayanov, by the KGB in Moscow after the collapse of the Soviet Union (Central Archive of the Ministry of State Security of the Russian Federation). Most of the letters have been made available from the previously closed archives of the so-called 'Prague Archiv' in Moscow. Vasilii Chayanov has published them, in Russian, in a biography of his father, *A.V. Chayanov – The Man, The Scholar, The Citizen*.
4. The Unified State Political Administration (secret police). Originally called CheKa, then GPU, then OGPU, then NKVD, then KGB.
5. In his study of the evolution of peasant farming (*Evolyutsiya i progress krest'yanskogo khozyaistva*), published in Moscow in 1923, Litoshenko compared the attraction of small-scale agriculture for Chayanov and his colleagues to the concepts of Narodniks in the late 1800s. G.A. Studenskii replied that Litoshenko had shown 'a total lack of taste' in coining the term 'Neonarodnik' [*Solomon*, 1977: 244]. For all that, the Bolsheviks themselves used the term in the official nomenclature of their own government – 'Narodnii Komissariat Zemledeliya (Narkomzem)', People's Commissariat of Agriculture.
6. People's (National) Commissariat for Agriculture. Chayanov joined the collegium in February 1921, as an adviser, and later also became the Narkomzem representative in Gosplan (State Organization for Planning).
7. New Economic Policy. After the extreme measures of 'War Communism', Lenin instituted a new policy, designed to mollify the peasantry. The official announcement was entitled: 'Report on the Substitution of a Tax in Kind for the Surplus Grain Appropriation System'.
8. The Moscow Popular University named for General A.L. Shanyavskii. In 1915, it was chosen as the location for an All-Russian Central Cooperative Committee. Active at Shanyavskii, in addition to Chayanov and Prokopovich, were A.E. Kulyzhnii, V.S. Zelgeim and M.I. Tugan-Baranovskii.
9. The Scientific Research Institute for Agricultural Economy and Agricultural Policy.
10. Tsentrosoyuz was organised in September, 1917, on the basis of the Moscow Regional Union of Consumer Societies, in which Chayanov held a prominent position. [*Balyazin*, 1990: 123].

11. On 14 January 1920, Lloyd George put a proposal before the Allied Supreme Economic Council to resume trade, not with the Soviet government, but with Tsentrosoyuz. The Council approved and, in Moscow, Tsentrosoyuz was immediately 'bolshevized', with the appointment of half a dozen high-ranking Bolsheviks to its controlling body, among them Krasin and Maksim Litvinov, who also were named to head a new trade delegation for talks with Britain [*O'Connor*, 1992: 233].

12. Other members of the commission that drew up the plan for a 'tax in kind' included Chayanov's colleague from his Institute, Nikolai Kondrat'ev, as well as members from the Commissariat, Ivan Teodorovich and Boris Knipovich.

13. Among Chayanov's early contacts with the Bolshevik regime was an experiment in co-operative organisation, in which a special commission was to be created within Narkomzem, to be called the 'Soviet of the Toiling Peasantry'. It was the accusation that he and his colleagues were the leaders of a counter-revolutionary 'Toiling Peasant Party' – that led to his prosecution as an 'enemy of the people' at the end of the decade of the 1920s.

14. A resolution of the Tenth Communist Party Congress, on 15 March 1921, ended the forced requisitioning of grain, and substituted a 'tax in kind' that permitted peasants to 'know how much tax was owed and when it was due' [*Heller*, 1986: 114–15].

15. 'A group of citizens of Idrissovsk division of the Zlatousk District officially petitioned the Divisional Executive District for permission to slaughter their children for food' [*Abramovitch*, 1962: 204–9]

16. Chayanov's name began to re-emerge from obscurity in the mid-1960s, not in Russia, but in the West, when R.E.F. Smith, working with Daniel Thorner and Basile Kerblay, translated his *Theory of Peasant Economy* into English. In 1976, *The Journal of Peasant Studies* published the full text of Chayanov's tale of the peasant utopia, translated into English by Professor Smith. It was originally published, in 1920, by the government's official press, Gosizdat. The preface was written and signed by a writer who also used a pseudonym, N. Orlovskii. Orlovskii really was the director of Gosizdat, Vatslav Vatslavovich Vorovskii, a talented writer and a favourite of Lenin's. Vorovskii duly noted the 'reactionary' point of view of the book, but indicated that it was worth reading. Vorovskii and Leonid Krasin were the two most active leaders urging Lenin to make use of technical experts like Chayanov. Both would be members of the delegation to the Genoa conference in 1922, and Vorovskii would be nominated in 1923 to succeed Krasin as Russia's diplomatic chief in London.

17. The Economic Conference (Ekoso), organised by Narkomzem in May 1921, met monthly under the leadership of I.A. Teodorovich and V.V. Osinskii. Members of the Praesidium were P.A. Mesyatsev, A.V. Chayanov and A.N. Morosanov [*Balyazin*, 1990: 138].

18. Fridtjof Nansen, Arctic explorer idolised by the Russians, including Lenin. He had been trying since 1919 to arrange humanitarian help for Russia. He co-operated closely with the American Relief operation and was in Moscow when the death sentences were announced.

19. The collegium of Narkomzem, meeting on 31 January 1922, discussed 'member of the collegium A.V. Chayanov', and 'the mission of comrade Chayanov to London at the disposal of Comrade Krasin'. The collegium decreed: '(1) to send comrade Chayanov to London at the disposal of comrade Krasin in April', and '(2) to assign for the mission of comrade Chayanov 5 thousand gold rubles to use for family support'. Also discussed was the question of 'agronomic emigrants'. The collegium decreed: '(1) to direct Chayanov, Mesyatsev and Shefler to discuss the question of the desirability of bringing back those agronomists who happen to be accidentally in Western Europe', and '(2) to direct comrade Chayanov to communicate with Narkomindel (the Commissariat of Foreign Affairs) about the return from abroad of professors Chelintsev and Makarov' [*RGAE*, f478, op. I, case 696, page 5]. (Both professors, close friends of Chayanov, had been working in the United States, Makarov with Professor George Frederick Warren at Cornell University and Chelintsev with Professor John Donald Black at Harvard.)

20. Alexsei Aleksandrovich Rybnikov (1887–1948), a painter, engraver and expert in restorations. He illustrated the *Hairdresser's Mannequin* by 'Botanik X', and used his own pseudonym, 'Antropolog A.'.

21. Both the Civil War, destructive as it was, and the 'foreign intervention', which never amounted to much, were history by 1921, when the famine began. The one factor in the

famine not attributable to the government was a severe drought, accompanied by forest and range fires,in the Volga region.

22. (Osnovy Selskokhoxiaistvennoi Politiki (tezisy) // Trudy 3-ego Vserossiiskogo S'ezda agronomov v Moske M, 1922 S. 13–14.

23. Professor Otto Georg Auhagen and Professor Max Zering. Both were well acquainted with Russian agriculture, had visited Russia on one or more occasions, and would see a good deal of Chayanov during his visit to Germany. It is highly probable that they were among the persons whom he visited in Berlin on his way to England.

24. Chayanov used one of his many pet names for his wife, Ol'ga, when he wrote, in this first letter: 'Lyolya hasn't been there (London) for a whole month.' Other variations included : 'O.-Em' in Letters 4, 'Lyushka', in Letters 8, 'O.E.' in Letters 10, 'Lyolina' and 'Olgina' in Letters 14, 'Olgunka' in Letters 15, 'Olei' in Letters 19, 'Olya' in Letters 20.

25. Russian history is replete with examples of internal exile within the country, and of voluntary exile abroad, but Lenin's action, at least in its scale, was something new. Maksim Gorkii accused Lenin of 'exterminating the intelligentsia in our illiterate country' [Heller, 1986: 140].

26. The 'Boyar's Palace' was just one street away from Chayanov's boyhood home.

27. Present-day residents of Hildenborough, when questioned, were astonished to learn that a prominent Russian scientist had lived in their village three-quarters of a century ago. Available records make no mention of '#3, New Council Cottages'. At least one Chayanov letter that has been preserved was mailed, not from Hildenborough, but from Tonbridge. Both are on the same rail line to London. Arrangements for Chayanov's accommodation would have been made, almost certainly, by Krasin's trade mission in London, or by the Tsentrosoyuz office in London. It would have been characteristic of Chayanov to request a place in the country. He did not like big cities. In his 1984 fantasy, Moscow was still Russia's largest city, but was limited to a population of 100,000. After his departure from England, he stayed only briefly in Berlin, then moved on, first to a small resort town near the Czech border, then to the university town of Heidelberg. On his return to Moscow, he settled down quite happily in an apartment at the Timiriazevskii Academy, on the outskirts of Moscow, continuing to live there until his arrest in 1930.

28. The reference to Nikolaevskii indicated that he was familiar with Yashchenko's friend and collabourator, Boris Nikolaevskii, and was aware that Nikolaevskii already was collecting materials for his archive. That archive was eventually housed at the Hoover Institution at Stanford University.

29. Prokopovich, with the help of the 'Russian Academic Group' of émigré scholars, set up an 'Economic Kabinet' in Berlin, a small-scale institute for Russian economic studies. When he and Kuskova left Berlin, his 'Kabinet' was transferred to Prague with him, sponsored by Czech President Masaryk's 'Action Russe' organisation.

30. The Genoa conference had failed to achieve its principal goals, and had been followed by a second ministerial conference in The Hague. This conference also produced little or nothing of value, other than a statement to the world press by Soviet Deputy Foreign Minister Litvinov that Russia had resumed grain exports to Western markets, while continuing to accept deliveries of food supplies from the American Relief Administration.

31. The 'House of Arts' met, from time to time, at a café-restaurant called the 'Loganhaus', at No.10 Kleiststrasse. Chayanov and his wife were scheduled to stay at a Pension called 'Hilma', at No.12 Kleiststrasse.

32. Chayanov's narrative ended with the sentence: 'End of First Part'. However, there was no 'Second Part,' and it is unclear whether Chayanov ever intended that there would be. There was, however, an odd appendage, a pretend newspaper called 'Zodii', dated 5 September 1984, carrying an essay by one of the story's chief characters, Aleksei Minin, named after Chayanov's close friend and colleague, Aleksandr Minin. The essay concluded: 'In the construction of Peasant Russia, we must develop – not freedom of government so much as freedom from government.'

33. Thomas More (1478–1535), English Utopian-socialist, introduced the term 'Utopia'; Edward Bellamy (1850–98), American author of socialist literature, including Looking Backward; Robert Blatchford (1851–1943), English socialist; Charles Fourier (1772–1837), French socialist-utopian.

34. Various theories have been put forward as to why Chayanov chose the year 1984 for his Utopia. It has been suggested that George Orwell, through his acquaintance with Evgenii Zamiatin, might have known about Chayanov's book, and have been aware of Chayanov's use of that year, but there is no factual material to indicate that the use of the same date by the two authors was anything but coincidental [*Smith*, 1981].

35. In an archival note ascribed to him, Chayanov pointed out that the letter 'X' can have two Russian pronunciations: if it is writen in the Latin alphabet, it's pronounced 'eex'; if it's in a cyrillic alphabet, it's pronounced 'kha'. He assumes that his pseudonym will be pronounced 'Botanik Kha' [*Chertkov, Sochinenia Botanik X*].

36. *The Venetian Mirror*, or *The Marvellous Adventures of the Glass People*.

37. Sylvester was mentor to the Awesome Ivan. He was in charge of the Tsar's household, and pioneered concepts of the family farm.

38. 'Albion', the ancient Celtic name for England.

39. There were, in fact, two Cousin Sokrats, the other being a cousin from his father's side, Sokrat Chayanov, also an agricultural scientist, who also would be arrested and imprisoned at the same time as Aleksandr. Klepikov was the closer of the two to Aleksandr.

40. In her monograph, *Torzhestvo Muz*, celebrating the 100th anniversary of the Bolshoi Theater, Ol'ga Chayanov expressed thanks to 'Mr. S. Wells' of Oxford University, for his help in establishing that there was a William Maddox in their registers for Merton College in 1752. Unfortunately, she was unable to make a firm connection with the Michael Yegorovich Maddox who built the 'Maddox Petrovsky Theatre' in the closing years of the eighteenth century.

41. *The History of the Hairdresser's Mannequin*, or *The Last Love of the Moscow, Architect M.* Published in the first year of the Republic (1918).

42. The Riesengebirge are in the area that, after the Second World War, was transferred from German to Polish control. Schreiberhau's Polish name is Szklarska Poreba. It is not far from Jelenia Gora, formerly Hirschberg, southeast of Berlin.

43. In the mid-1930s, while he was in prison, Chayanov made what he considered an 'extraordinary' advance in the use of correlations, developing what he called 'functional dependence of methods of statistical grouping'.

44. The initials of the first secret police organization of the Bolshevik government were the letter 'CH' (pronounced Che) and the letter 'K' (pronounced Ka) – CHrezvichainaia Komissiia/ Extraordinary Commission (for the Struggle Against Counterrevolution and Sabotage). Agents of the CHeKa were known as Chekists.

45. The 'institute' in question might have been Prokopovich's 'Economic Cabinet', but it is more likely to have been the 'Russian Institute' that Prokopovich had helped to organise in Berlin.

46. Elena Vasilevna Grigoreva, Chayanov's 'first love', and first wife, whom he married just before his departure on a European trip in 1912. The residence on Degtiarnii Pereulok appears to have been assigned to Chayanov through the auspices of the Sverdlov Communist University, where Chayanov taught for a time. The address was 'Degtiarnii Pereulok, House 13, Apartment 2 on the courtyard'.

47 . The use of 'faith healers' has always been popular in Russia. Sokrat's problem appears to have been a form of eczema.

48. In the 'Sovnarkom' archive, a small document attrests to the receipt from Chayanov of 'Materials for Agricultural Concessions and other purposes, prepared for the Genoa Conference'. It is signed by Fridrikhson, 3 II 23, Berlin.

49. The Russian word 'tolstyi' means 'thick' or 'fat'. When applied to books or journals it means 'serious'.

50 'Gegenwartiger Stand der landwirtschaftlichen Ökonomik in Russland' // Schmoller's Jahrbuch, 1922: 46, 73; 'Die neueste Entwicklung des Agrarökonomik in Russland' // *Archiv für Sozialwissenschaft und Sozialpolitik'; Tübingen*. 1923. 50.

51. 'Moi priyatel'.

52. 'tyozka'.

53. This work is commonly listed in English as: 'On the Theory of Non-Capitalist Economic Systems', although the German translation from which the English is usually derived reads: 'Zur Frage einer Theorie der Nichtkapitalistischen Wirtschaftssysteme', and the word 'zur',

a contraction of 'zu der', ordinarily is translated as 'to', not 'on'. Since the reference, in this instance, is in a letter written by Chayanov himself, it seems appropriate to use a literal translation of his Russian text: 'K voprosu o Ekonomicheskoi teorii nekapitalisticheskikh sistem narodnogo khoziaistva'. (If he had intended to say 'On' or 'About', he would have written 'O voprosom'.) The grammatical construction appears to indicate that his emphasis was more on the formulation of theory than on assessment of systems. Solomon suggests that the article was written in German, and notes that 'the reasons why Chayanov chose to publish this seminal work in German remain obscure' [*Solomon*, 1977: 49, 225n]. This letter appears to clarify that uncertainty. Chayanov does not appear to have written the article in German. His command of German and French was excellent, quite sufficient for writing letters, but on scientific matters, he thought and wrote in Russian. One may presume that he published the article in German because he had an offer of publication from a German periodical, just as he published his 1923 book on the Peasant Economy in German because he had a German publisher willing to publish it. The article concerning Non-Capitalist systems did appear in Russian in 1989 [A.V. *Chayanov*, 1989].

54. Abram Grigorevich Vishnyak (1895–1943), editor and director of 'Gelikon' publishing house, which began in Moscow in 1918 and moved to Berlin in 1921.

55. Wrangltsi' – followers of Baron Peter Wrangel, a staunch monarchist, one of the last holdouts in the civil war against the Bolsheviks; 'Cadets' – members of the Konstitutional Democrat faction; 'Eser of Chernovskii doctrine' – Socialist-Revolutionaries loyal to Viktor Chernov; 'Eser of Kerenskii doctrine' – Socialist-Revolutionaries loyal to Alexander Kerenskii.

56. A document included in Chayanov's KGB archive is a copy of a report from the French police, apparently related to the request by Chayanov and his wife for permission to travel to Western Europe in 1927. The purpose of the trip was described as: 'going to France for 2 months to study French agriculture, wine, horticulture in the south, linen production in the north'. The document described 'the wife' as being an envoy of the Commissariat of Enlightenment. It also described 'the wife' as 'Ol'ga, born 4 January, 1897, in Paris. Writer'.

57. The Scientific Research Institute for Agrarian Economy and Agrarian Policy, of which he was the director.

58. Nikolai Nikolaievich Krestinskii, former member of Lenin's Politburo and Commissar of Finance, who became the first USSR ambassador to Germany after the agreement in Rapallo in 1922.

59. Aleksandr Aleksandrovich Nikonov, as president of the All-Russian Academy of Agricultural Science, was the person most responsible for securing the rehabilitation in 1987 of Chayanov and his fellow victims of the 'Toiling Peasant Party' prosecution.

60. His output to the world was broken, but he continued to work. In his letter of 4 June 1931 [*OGPU*: 175], to the OGPU Secret Political Department, 2nd Section, he wrote: 'At the present time I submit the following information about the status of my scientific papers and the current status of my scientific work, supposing that this might have significance for a different direction in the conditions of my punishment.' He then outlined five projects on which he had been working in prison:

(1) Methods of planning large-scale enterprises of socialist agriculture.
(2) Calculation and methods of determining the effectiveness of socialist agriculture.
(3) Organisation of water and southern agriculture in general.
(4) Analysis of the possibility of disclosure not only of correlation, but also functional dependence of methods of statistical grouping.
(5) Historic topography of Moscow and its regions.

Chayanov wrote that he considered his work in prison on Item #4 to be 'extraordinary'. He suggested that it would be 'inexpedient to leave these works unfinished and unpublished'.

3

Letters

Edited and Translated by

FRANK BOURGHOLTZER

There are 41 letters in the collection: from Chayanov–39; from Gorkii–1; from Kuskova–1.

The recipients of Chayanov's letters are : 7 to S.N. Prokopovich; 6 to E.D. Kuskova; 1 to Kuskova and Prokopovich; 12 to Sokrat Klepikov; 3 to Aleksandr Yashchenko; 1 to Gennadi Studenskii; 1 to Narkomzem; 1 to Professor E. Laur; 5 to Aleksandr Baxrax. In addition there are 2 autographs to Baxrax. The letter from Gorkii is to Kuskova; the letter from Kuskova is to Vera Figner.

Asterisks designate originals bearing dates.

Question marks designate approximate dates for originals not bearing dates.

	Date	From	To	Addressed to:
			1922	
1	? May, 1922	Kent	Moscow (?)	Prokopovich
2	* 1 June	Moscow (Kuskova)	Moscow (?)	Figner
3	* 30 June	Berlin (Gorkii)	Berlin	Kuskova
4	? June	Hildenborough	Moscow	Sokrat
5	* 20.VII.22	Hildenborough	Berlin	Yashchenko
6	* 12-13.VIII.22	England	Berlin	Kuskova
7	* 13.VIII.22	Tonbridge	Berlin	Yashchenko
8	? September	England	Berlin	Kuskova
9	* 24 IX 22	England	Moscow	Sokrat
10	? September	Kent	Moscow	Sokrat
11	* 22.X.22	Kent	Moscow	Sokrat
12	? December	Berlin	Moscow	Sokrat
13	Pre-Christmas	Schreiberhau	Berlin	Prokopovich
14	Pre-Christmas	Schreiberhau	Berlin	Kuskova

Date	From	To	Addressed to:

1923

	Date	From	To	Addressed to:
15	* 2 Jan. 1923	Mittelschreiber	Moscow	Sokrat
16	* 3 I 23	Schreiberhau	Berlin	Prokopovich
17	* 18.I.23	Mittelschreiberhau	Berlin	Yashchenko
18	? January	Schreiberhau	Moscow	Sokrat
19	? February	Schreiberhau	Moscow	Sokrat
20	? February	Schreiberhau	Moscow	Sokrat
21	? February	Schreiberhau	Moscow	Sokrat
22	* 2 March	Schreiberhau	Moscow	Sokrat
23	* 13.III.23	Berlin	Berlin	Baxrax: a, Autograph
24	* 14.III.23	Berlin	Berlin	Baxrax: b, Autograph
25	? March	Heidelberg	Berlin	Kuskova
26	* 18.IV.23	Heidelberg	Berlin	Prokopovich
27	? April	Heidelberg	Berlin	Baxrax: 1
28	? May	Heidelberg	Moscow	Sokrat
29	? May	Heidelberg	Berlin	Baxrax: 2
30	* 8 May 1923	Heidelberg	Berlin	Baxrax: 3
31	* 22 May	Heidelberg	Berlin	Baxrax: 4
32	* 2 June	Heidelberg	Berlin	Baxrax: 5
33	? 15 June	Heidelberg	Moscow	NKZ
34	? June	Heidelberg	Moscow	Studenskii
35	? July	Heidelberg	Berlin	Prokopovich
36	? July	Heidelberg	Berlin	Kuskova
37	* 10 August 23	Heidelberg	Berlin	Prokopovich
38	? July/August	Heidelberg	Berlin	Kuskova
39	* 21 August	Heidelberg	Zurich, Switzerland	Prof. Laur
40	* 10 Sept	Heidelberg	Berlin	Prokopovich
41	1927	Paris	Prague	E.D. and S.N.

SOURCES

Letters 1, 4, 6, 8, 9, 10, 11, 12, 13, 14, 15, 16, 18, 19, 20, 21, 22, 25, 26, 28, 34, 35, 36, 37, 38, 39, 40, 41
    Chayanov, V.A. [1998]
Letters 23, 24, 27, 29, 30, 31, 32
    Baxrax [1982].
Letters 3, 5, 7, 17
    Fleishman , Hughes and Raevsky-Hughes [1983].
Letter 33
    Nikonov [1989].
Letter 2
    Leontiev [1993].

Letter 1

Undated (?May, 1922).[1] From Kent. To Prokopovich.

Dear Sergei Nikolaevich!

I am writing you at this time an economics letter, in connection with my current work on the peasant economy. I want very much not to parallel your work on the derivation of correlation coefficients, but rather to simplify them in support of my next chapter. Therefore, I would very much like to ask you to tell me what information you have about the printing of your book in Moscow, and, if it has appeared, or will appear, then to ask you, if you can, to send me one copy when you receive it, if only temporarily.

And, for the same purpose, if you have the numbers at hand or in memory, I would very much like to ask you to send me the coefficients of correlation between Family (C[onsumer] or W[orker] or P[erson], all the same) = Farming Income; Family = Gross Income (Farming plus Crafts and Trades).

In my theoretical view, the correlation relating Fam = Gr Inc (Farm + Cr-Tr) should give a higher coefficient than Fam = Ag Inc.

It is very hard to work without books. I have not been able to find a whole range of budgets, and above all, not one book with an analysis of the social structure of the peasant farm for materials repeating the census material of Chernenkov, Kryashcheva, Vikhlyaev, Kushchenko and others. Perhaps, by chance, you have them.

We are living peacefully. We read Leskova[2] study the English dialect and go walking on the rare occasions when it isn't raining. London, I still haven't explored, and Lyolya[3] hasn't been there for a whole month. The hardest of all is to get used to English cooking ... bad food, and terrible wine of an unknown sort.

Nonetheless, there is a not bad Madeira – for holiday drinking.

Greetings.

A. Chayanov

NOTES

1. Presumably addressed to Prokopovich in Moscow, before his banishment. Chayanov could not have known that Kuskova and Prokopovich had left Russia until some time after their departure on 1 June. Chayanov, who left Russia on 6 April, appears to have been in England for something more than a month.
2. Nikolai Semenovich Leskov (1831–95), a writer known for his skill in creating characters, his style and his use of language. A favorite of Chayanov's.
3. Nickname for Ol'ga Emmanuilovna, Chayanov's wife.

Letter 2

June 1, 1922 From Kuskova to Figner. Moscow
Moscow, I VI 1922

Dear Vera Nikolaevna!

Today, we leave to go abroad. As hard as we tried to organize our behavior so that, here in our homeland, we might endure the revolution – (we were) unsuccessful. Now, our task is different – not to become emigrants. This, for me, personally, I think, and also for SN – psychologically impossible. But the mistrust of our authorities is so great and so painful that there will undoubtedly be pushing to one side from the other. From our own side, there will be, in opposition, a stubborn, persistent desire to return to our homeland. In a word – mired down in argument. It would be nice to become the winner. Undoubtedly, on the subject of our current departure, the truth is that a great, a very great role was played by you and Ek Pav Pav.[1] Without you both, it would have come to this, that we would have continued, with no redeeming features, in a life of work in Kashin or in some other similar place. Permit me, dear sweet Vera Nikolaevna, warmly and from our hearts, to thank you for your efforts.[2] This gratitude comes from a pure heart and long will live in it. May you have only good health, prosperity and the opportunity to take a holiday. I promise you to rest – as best I can.

Warmest greetings to Ev Nik and Mix Pet.[3]

Loving you, Ek Kuskova-Prokopovich

Dear Vera Nikolaevna, very sorry not to see you in Moscow before our departure abroad. I will await you there. Periodically Russian citizens must rest from the smoke of the fatherland, otherwise the eyes corrode. Therefore, may you be good and healthy and do not forget the expulsion from Russia of this debater of yours.

S. Prokopovich

NOTES

1. Ekaterina Pavlovna Peshkova, the first wife of Maksim Gorkii (A.M. Peshkov). A former Socialist Revolutionary, she served from 1918 to 1937 as leader of the Moscow Committee of the Political Red Cross. Vera Figner was an honorary member of the Red Cross. Figner, and Gorkii, were members of the Committee to Aid the Hungry.
2. Shortly before the expulsion of Kuskova and Prokopovich, Kuskova wrote to Figner, thanking her for speaking to Kamenev on their behalf. Sergei Kamenev was one of Lenin's top colleagues, and had been chairman of the Committee to Aid the Hungry. The Committee had been created at Kuskova's suggestion, based on a proposal she had submitted to Kamenev.
3. Evgenia Nikolaevna Sazhina was the younger sister of Vera Figner, married to Mikhail Petrovich Sazhin.

Letter 3

30 June, 1922. From Maksim Gorkii in Berlin to Kuskova

Dear Ekaterina Dmitrievna!

Your arrival is not surprising, since I knew already in April of the decision to banish all the members of the committee from Russia.

What are thinking of doing? Probably, you would like to write, – have you not talked about this with Grzhebin?[1] You probably know that he and Martov[2] are in charge of the publication – 'Archive of the Russian Revolution.' Certainly you and Serg. Nik.[3] could offer a great deal to this publication.

(Gorkii's letter has been reconstituted from fragments in Heller [1991] and Fleishman, Hughes and Raevsky-Hughes [1983].

VMESTO SMERTNOI KAZNI Heller [1992: 3. col 3].

Reshenie o primennii novoi karatelnoi mery bylo priiatno, vidimo, vesnoi '1922 g. Kogda E. Kuskova priexala – vyslannaya – v Berlin, ona poluchila pismo ot Gorkogo, vyekhavshego iz sovestskoi Rossii v Oktyabre 1921 g. On pisal: 'Dorogaya Ekaterina Dmitrievna! Priezdom vashim ne udivlen, ibo esche v aprele znal, chto vsekh chlenov komiteta resheno vyselit iz Rossii'. (E.D. Kuskova. 'Tragediya Maksima Gorkogo'. *Novyi Zhurnal*, 38, 1954. str. 237)

RUSSKII BERLIN 1921 1923 Fleishman, Hughes and Raevsky-Hughes [1983: 368–69].

Arkhiv zhurnala – Letopis' Revolyutsii v Kollektsii Nikolaevskogo (No 1280, Box 2). 30 Iyunia 1922 g. Gorkii pishet E D. Kuskovoi, tol'ka chto vyslannoi iz Sovetskoi Rossii; 'Chto dumaete delat? Veroyatno, u vas est' okhota pisat, – ne pogovorit' li vam po etomu povodu s Grzhebinym? Vy, veroyatno, znaete, chto on zatevaet s Martovym vo glave izdanie – 'Arkhiv russkoi revoliutsii'. Uveren, chto vy i Serg Nik mogli by mnogo dat' etomu izdaniyu' (E.D. Kuskova. 'Tragediia Maksima Gorkogo'. *Novyi Zhurnal*, 38, 1954. str. 237)

NOTES

1. Z.I. Grzhebin, under the patronage of Maksim Gorkii, started a publishing house in Petrograd with the initial purpose of publishing historical material about the revolution. When it became clear that they would publish works by revolutionary leaders who had been opponents of the Bolsheviks, Grzhebin found it expedient to move his publishing house to Berlin. Gorkii also became a 'semi-émigre' in Berlin, and work proceeded on their 'Archive of the Russian Revolution.'

2. Yulii Martov (Yulii Osipovich Tsederbaum, 1873–1923), Socialist Democrat from the earliest times, became an 'internationalist', a 'left menshevik'. Emigrated in 1920. Started the newspaper *Sotsialisticheskii Vestnik (Socialist Courier)* in Berlin.

3. Sergei Nikolaevich (Prokopovich).

Letter 4

?June, 1922. From Kent. To Sokrat.

A. Tchayanoff
3 New Consil Cottages
Hildenborough, Kent, England

Dear Sokrat!

I write you, it seems, already a third letter from England, and urgently request you to reply.

First of all, about what is happening with the Boyar's Palace.[1] I have written dozens of letters, beginning with Narkom, ending with Marosanov[2] and, other than official telegrams from Yakovenko,[3] have received nothing in reply from anybody.

Secondly, about what is happening with the Supreme Seminars, a letter tells me that N.D.[4] has parked himself in apartments there, and has thrown our students out of three rooms. This is something beyond reality, and all the more reason for me to ask for information.

In general, according to reports coming from Moscow, and letters, I have arrived at the conclusion that our 'professor',[5] since my departure, has become angry about absolutely everything related to me and my name, and is taking very indelicate steps to defile my good name.

I would like to receive information from you also in this connection. And in addition, tell me, has the Petrovka academy really made him a 'professor', or is he signing 'prof.' under his name in the *Bulletin of the Conjuncture Institute* because of naive vanity?

Enough of this!

We went looking for your mystery books in Paris and in London, and didn't find any.[6]

A. Chayanov.

P.S. O. Em[7] sends regards.

P.P.S. It would be rather nice, if you all found a minute to visit at Plyushchikh street with the offspring of Belyankin.

Listen, if you find the time, please 'remingtonirovat'[8] from the encyclopedia the words of the article 'Musyka', that a lady here promises to send to her sister. Write.

NOTES

1. Chayanov wanted his Scientific Research Institute for Agrarian Economy and Agrarian Policy to be housed in a splendid palace that was built for the Boyar Volkov in the eighteenth century on Great Kharitonevskii Lane, in Moscow. The aristocratic Yusupov family later occupied the palace. Chayanov succeeded in establishing his Institute in this boyar's palace after his return from Europe in 1923. His Institute virtually disappeared in 1928, when it was incorporated into a Stalinized National Research Institute. Chayanov lost his title of 'director' but was retained as a member of the collegium, kept his office in the 'boyar's palace' and was working there as an advisor on the development of State farms in 1930, when he was arrested.

2. Aleksei Nikolaevich Marosanov, economist, agronomist. He was in charge of Narkomzem publications, and manager of the agricultural journal, *Novaya Derevnya*.
3. Yakovenko, an official of Narkomzem.
4. Nikolai Dmitrievich Kondrat'ev was a close collaborator with Chayanov in the development of theories of cooperation. When Chayanov set up his research institute for agriculture, Kondrat'ev became its most prominent member, after Chayanov. In short order, Kondrat'ev, with Chayanov's help, set up a subsidiary institute for the study of economics and market relationships. When Chayanov began his European trip, Kondrat'ev became the de-facto leader of both institutes. There seems to have been, in fact, a love-hate relationship beteween Chayanov and Kondrat'ev
5. Kondrat'ev.
6. Both Chayanov and Sokrat were deeply interested in occult (mystery) matters .
7. Chayanov's wife, Ol'ga Emanuilovna.
8. Type out.

Letter 5

20.VII.22   From Hildenborough. To Yashchenko

Dear Aleksandr Semenovich!

Yesterday I sent you a whole pile of agricultural literature from my trunks, which finally arrived in London.

I very much ask, in return, special consideration for all the periodical publications, that when you have them reviewed, they should first be read through to the end. That will be instructive and interesting. From the books , I ask your indulgence concerning the review of Nikitin's book, ('O s.x.raionax Mosk. Gub.').[1] After all of our trials, we've only just settled down in England and I think that soon I'll be sending you others of the things I promised.

My address: A. Tschayanoff, 3 New Council Cottages, Hildenborough, Kent, England, to where I hope, in exchange for the package, to receive No. 6 and succeeding N.R.K.'s.

Greetings!

A. Chayanov.

P.S. Thanks! for your review on 'Botanik X.!'.[2]

If you please, on the expiration date of S-X Zhizn'(Agricultural Life) and others ,please don't throw them on the shelf or give them to Nikolaevsky to cut up (rezat'), but send them to the care of S.N. Prokopovich.

NOTES

1. N.P. Nikitin was a participant in Chayanov's High-level seminars which developed into his Research Institute. The book was actually entitled Divisions of the Agricultural Region of Moscow Guberniya., and it was not reviewed, but Chayanov referred to it in the book he was writing.
2. Three of Chayanov's romantic tales – Venediktov, The story of the Hairdresser's Mannequin and The Cheaters – using his pseudonym 'Botanik X' – were mentioned and would be reviewed in the first issue of NRK in 1923.

Letter 6

12 .VIII. 22.   From England to Kuskova.

Dear Ekaterina Dmitrievna!

Your letter received, and I thank you very much for it, even though I don't measure up to that first line about '… my high communist assignment', and I fear that Moscow gossip, now, will be in the form of rumors that I've had a rapprochement with Burtsev or Chernov.[1]

A substantive answer to your letter is very difficult for me, since I don't have at my disposal a hundredth part of the rich information which you enjoy. From Moscow, I receive only letters from relatives. I conclude from these letters that people live variously, either well or very poorly, and that in northern Russia the harvest is not bad, but in the south it's bad again.

I have nothing more profound than this to offer, since I don't even read the English newspapers every day.

As to what should be done – in the absence of infomative material, it's difficult to say. I suppose that each of us should do whatever seems right, seems appropriate, and this is how I see your present mission: to put it simply, you intend to publish a genuine Russian newspaper.

If I understand your task correctly as an effort to bring an end to the civil division, to transform the Russian problem from one of struggle against the regime to one of redemption and re-birth of the homeland, with all its existing forces, including the communists, so long as they have a living, creative origin – then success, if it's granted, would be for you an extraordinary, historic work, and, properly speaking, it's unlikely that anyone other than you could undertake such a task. Nobody can reproach you for partisanship, and the position which you occupy now is, basically, that which you held in 1917, as judged by your wonderful speeches in the Pre-Parliament.[2]

If you are interested in my opinion on the character that would be desirable in your newspaper, I would say that you should run it just as you would do it in today's Moscow, if a free press existed there now.

I agree completely that such an organ would carry extraordinary weight and authority, especially amidst today's emigré press, which constantly sings the 'Internationale' topsy-turvy:

'We the whole Soviet world will destroy
To its foundation, and then, we will … etc. etc.

and continues to include, as even *Poslednie Novosti*[3] sometimes does in its general information, military secrets, albeit involving the Red army, but it's still the Russian national army.

My nearest plans for the year in terms of urgency are of a strictly scientific character: to establish a scientific foundation for my basic social beliefs. Concretely – I have succeeded in producing already a rough draft of 3 large chapters of 'Peasant Economy'. I'm working now on the 4th, and there are about 10 still to come.

Very keenly do I feel my shortage of Russian books and I await with great impatience the publication of Sergei Nikolaevich's last work about peasant budgets, concerning which I am writing to him in person.

As for London, I go there seldom, and I solemnly adhere to your advice not to refuse a single conversation when one is requested, but not to initiate one myself. Thus it was that I had a short meeting with Braikevich and Buryshkin 4 , agreeing with the first on all points.

And that's all! Would be very glad to see you in London. Life here is quiet and very peaceful.

A. Chayanov. 13.VIII.22

The Utopia I banish, the pseudonym I seldom unveil![5]

NOTES

1. Viktor Chernov was a founder of the Socialist Revolutionary Party and became Minister of Agriculture in the Provisional government after the first revolution of 1917. V. L. Burtsev was a member of the Cadet faction and a leader in the development of evidence purporting to show that Lenin and the Bolsheviks were subsidized by the German government. Both went to Berlin after the revolution, Chernov to found a major émigré newspaper, *Golos Rossii* (*The Voice of Russia*), and Burtsev to collaborate on the Cadet émigrés' newspaper, *Rul'* (The Helm).
2. After the Bolshevik seizure of power, the future form of government was to be decided by a Constituent Assembly. To prepare this Assembly, a conference was held, called the 'Pre-Parliament', for which both Kuskova and Chayanov were chosen as delegates.
3. *Poslednie Novosti* (Latest News) was the principal Russian emigré newspaper in Paris, edited and published by historian Pavel Milyukov, one of the most respected anti-Bolshevik socialists.
4. Mikhail Vladimirovich Braikevich, economist, engineer, follower of Milyukov; P.A. Buryshkin, author of works on philosophy and religion.
5. Chayanov worried a great deal about the possibility that he would have political problems because of his utopian book of economic- science fiction, *The Journey of my Brothe, Alexei to the Land of the Peasant Utopia*. It was published under the pseudonym of 'Ivan Kremnev'. Presumably Kuskova made some mention of it in the letter Chayanov had just received.

Letter 7

13.VIII.22   From Tonbridge to Yashchenko

Aleksandr Semenovich! dearest friend!

Huge thanks to you for No. 6 of NRK and your letter, and I have a great favor to ask of you: if you are going to print a review of the Kremnev utopia, I urgently ask that the pseudonym not be unveiled and, as to the 'historical part' and all the prognoses of historical sequences, this doesn't apply as much, but, since the unveiling of the pseudonym in No. 5[1] has already cost me very dearly, I don't wish to pour oil on the fire.

Greetings!

A. Chayanov

NOTE

1. The issue #5 of *Novaya Russkaya Kniga*, which appeared in June of 1922, carried a notice about Chayanov that stated: 'At the beginning of 1920, there appeared in Moscow (Gosizdat) under the pseudonym of Ivan Kremnev the first part of *Puteshestvie moego brata Alekseya v stranu krest'yanskoi utopii.*'

Letter 8

From England to Kuskova

Dear Ekaterina Dmitrievna!

Things are not so good with us. Lyushka has been on her back, in bed, for a week already: headache and languor. The doctor, as yet, has not examined her seriously for the possibility that she is expecting a little one, but he seems to think that her illness is normal for this land. It would be good if that turns out to be the case. I am also beginning to feel somewhat out of sorts. The first chance we get, we'll abandon the fogs of Albion, and we are thinking about going to Italy, by way of Berlin, where she can undergo a fundamental, all-around medical analysis.. An appendicitis operation, it seems, should also be done by the Germans, since we have been advised not to have it done here in England, where the cost of such a pleasure would be around 150 pounds.

To the extent that my health permits, I have begun work on the subject of the peasant economy and, thanks to the kindness of my Moscow friends, I received from Moscow a few days ago almost all my missing books.

The only thing I'm lacking is the correlation coefficient from the work of S.N.,[1] but evidently the publication of his book has been postponed.

Would be very grateful to you, if you could tell me about the final fate of A.A. Rybnikov and N.D. Kondrat'ev,[2] and also where abroad the Osorgins, Matveev, Lyubimov and Sigirskii[3] have settled down.

Lyolya is especially interested in M.A.[3] I, for more than a week now, have been cut off from all the world and, other than what is in the newspapers, know nothing of what is happening.

Letters , not only from Moscow but even from Berlin, finish the most interesting parts laconically, with the words: '… will tell you about this in detail when we meet in person'.

The censorship is not only Russian. Even the English have become devilishly strict and, for example, a letter from Paris came to me unsealed.

Well – So long and all the best.

A Ch.

NOTES

1. Prokopovich.
2. Rybnikov and Kondrat'ev were two of the closest colleagues of Chayanov. Both had been arrested as members of the anti-hunger committee, but were not subjected to exile.
3. Mikhail Andreevich Osorgin: Russian writer, author of *Sivtsev Vrazhek* (published in English as *Quiet Street.*), wrote for Kuskova's newspapers, served with her on the Famine Committee, was one of the Committee members, including Kuskova, sentenced to death, then to internal exile, then to exile abroad. L.A. Matveev: economist, held a high post in the Ministry of Finance prior to the revolution. D.N. Lyubimov: civil servant under Tsarist rule, active in application of the Stolypin reforms. After the revolution, he opened an antique shop in Petrograd. Sigorskii was an activist in the Russian co-operative movement.

Letter 9

24.IX.22   From England   To Sokrat

Dear Sokrat!

I received your long letter and have already answered it. Publication of your atlas of bank-notes of the epoch of war and revolution, in my opinion, is not possible for two reasons.

1) Foreign publishing houses publish here only fast-selling, cheap books of fiction with fanatical black hundreds content and current political profile literature. Your book is serious. At the same time, my connections with book publishers here are so weak that I am unable, despite all my efforts, to place in the Russian language even one of my books and I can only settle for a German publication of 'Kooperation' and 'Optimal size'. Russian publishers in England – none at all.

2) Collecting of bank-notes here is expanding nicely and they say that collections exist of up to 800-1000 examples. In English quality (marochnyx) shops they are selling bank-notes from the epoch of the Civil War – thus I fear that your collection is too incomplete for publication. In any case, I will write to Ladyzhnikov in Berlin, to ask him to seek out publishers and attempt to get in touch with some collectors, to learn from them about the state of affairs here.

Yesterday, through the agricultural agent of Vneshtorg, Zherebtsov, I forwarded to you the *Histoire philosophique* of Olivet[1] (price, 30 shillings/ 60 million sov. rubles), and another, as I already wrote to you, still more expensive, 3 or 4 pounds. Zherebtsov is sending them to NKZ, to the attention of Knipovich. Together with the books are going a dress for mama and several things for Olina's father and Melissa. Please arrange to have them delivered.

I beseech you to send me, even though temporarily, Kushchenko (I don't remember the title),[2] the book about the dynamic of the peasant farms of Surazhskii uezd and the work of the subsection on statistics at the Congress of Natural Scientists and Physicians, along with the articles of Arnol'd[3] on mathematical elaboration of sowing groups (both are in my book-case at Nikolopeskovskii pereulok).[4] Give Knipovich the message that the books he sent have arrived, and many thanks.

Enclosed, I am sending 8 wood engravings of portraits from the XVI century, of which the dearest and earliest have red stripes on the reverse side. I found in London quite a few views of Moscow, engravings and drawings.

Very assiduously and very successfully, I am writing my book on the peasant economy.

So long.

A. Chayanov.

P.S. Please ... send me in return for Olivet all numbers of *Sredi Kollektsionerov* (*Among Collectors*) that have come out in my absence.

NOTES

1. Antoine Fabre d'Olivet (1768–1825).
2. Georgii Aleksandrovich Kushchenko (1878– ...). Developed methods of dynamic analysis of the peasant economy.

3. Vladimir Fedorovich Arnol'd (1878– ...), economist, statistician. His theories strongly
    influenced Chayanov.
4. Chayanov's Institute, at this time, still was housed in a small mansion on Great
    Nikolopeskovskii lane, just off the Arbat in Moscow.

Letter 10

?September, 1922   From Kent to Sokrat

Dear Sokrat!

Hereby I inform you, that on 28.X.22 we intend to leave Kent and advance on Italy through Berlin until 15.XI.22. Our address – Pen 'Hilma' 12, Kleiststrasse.[1]

O.E. sends a personal letter.

NOTE

1. The original letter appears to read 'Klein' strasse, but it is probable that Kleiststrasse was intended.

Letter 11

22/X/22   From Kent   To Sokrat

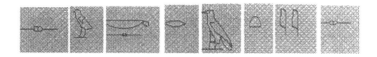

Dear Sokrat!

Pictured above is hieroglyphic type that I borrowed from the British museum, and it means your name – Sokrates..

I advise you to use it for your press and stamps. I must report to you that my wife, Ol'ga Emmanuilovna, while visiting local antiquarians, found a special Egyptian store, where they deal in scarabs, prints, (Azirisami, Izidami) and so forth and for financial reasons call themselves 'the Egyptian museum of the 4th dynasty', but after being engrossed in engravings because of their great cheapness we now both already possess 'collections' in which are included Rembrant, Durer, Beham, Altdorfer and others, and, like a pearl (i perlom yavlyaet'sya), L. Collot 'Personnages of Italian Comedy', but what pleases her most of all is a certain Roman composition, a maddening either Aldeg< ... >, or Aleart Classen – we leave the decision to your competent judgment in Moscow..

However, I must report that engravings here are very expensive, more expensive than in Moscow, (and) they must be bought not at an antiquary, where their price is one or two pounds apiece, but at a junk dealer of a (nerazobranni) and uncertain type. So much for that!

This letter to you is the last from England. The other day, we received Italian visas and we are going to Rome with a stopover in Berlin, where I must meet with Osinskii.

Write.

Did you receive my 'Occult Dyadyu' and engravings? Until later. Farewell

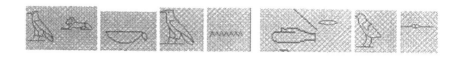

alexsandros

Letter 12

?December   From Berlin   To Sokrat

My dear Sokrat!

Fate has fittingly punished you for laziness. If you had written to me in timely fashion about your visa difficulties, I could have made it easy for you. Now though, alas, it is late, because this business takes 2–3 weeks. To prolong a transit visa through Germany is extremely difficult. Therefore, we must make every effort to receive an entry or a transit with a month or 2-weeks' stay, since Prague does nothing either for your children or for your treatment.

I believe that, if you can show the German consulate a certificate from Kiselev, saying that your eczema requires consultation with Dr. Paul Krouse (Berlin) or Prof. Krehl (Heidelberg). you will be allowed a stay of two weeks in transit. At any rate, I am not mistaken in thinking that, even with a transit visa good for five days, you and I could meet, if only on the train platform, either in Berlin or Dresden. I do think that in Saxony it would be possible to prolong a transit visa, although with a smaller chance of success.

In Berlin, I advise you to stay either in the Hotel Russicher Hof (right across from the railway station on Friedrichstrasse) or the Hotel am Zoo near the Bahnhof Zoologischer Garten on Kurfurst. You must send a telegram in advance.

Help with your visa et cetera might be rendered by Sergei Ivanovich Salovri of Zentrosojus[1] (Tsentrosoyuz), and through him N.I. Lyubimov at Unter den Linden 17–18, 3rd etage (by … 4 etage) and, with Narkomzem, Fridrikhson, M.A. Lebedeva, A.V. Sobashnikov, at Liezenburgerstr. 11 (this is near Kurfurstendam).

From Riga, send a telegram. I will respond through Zentrosoyuz (Salovri), who, in general, functions as my Berlin representative.

Just in case I will give you some addresses of engraving shops:

Berlin:
> Near the Fridrichstrasse Banhof
> Amsler & Ruthardt, Behrenstr. 29a or 27?
> Also a store two or three houses from there, on the same side, near

Kurfurstendam:
> Hollstein and Pupper, Meinikestr. 19, in the courtyard
> Both very expensive.

Dresden
> Franz Meyer. Hohestr. 4, in the courtyard

I very much want to know from one of the following persons: Fantalov, Mesyatsev, Rybnikov or prof. Villiams,[2] the status of my apartment in Petrovka and, using their influence on special points, report to me in detail.

Aunt Ol'ga sends the instruction to you to discuss with your former most gentle nanny, if she won't agree to become our nanny and governess.

Greetings! Write! Least of all must you worry about money – for you there will always be work.

NOTES

1. 'Zentrosojus' in the text.
2. Sergei Ivanovich Fantalov, secretary of the faculty of agricultural economy and policy at the Petrovskii Academy; Mesyatsev, member of the collegium of Narkomzem and Narkomzem representative with Narkompros (Commissariat of Enlightenment); Vasilii Robertovich Villiams, chairman of the statistical cathedra at Petrovskii/Timiryazevskii Academy from 1920-28; Aleksandr Aleksandrovich Rybnikov, one of Chayanov's closest colleagues. The Petrovskii Academy was under the control of the Commissariat of Enlightement

Letter 13

Pre-Christmas, 1922.   From Schreiberhau to Prokopovich

Dear Sergei Nikolaevich!

Huge thanks to you for your Vologodskii collection, which I can get back to you in 2 or 3 days. We have as guests the Makarov family, who made their way to us with exceptional courage, passing through mountain snow drifts, changing trains 8 times and doing 20 versts on horseback through the snow to get here from Prag. Snow has been falling for a whole week without stopping and we can get around only by following paths through the snow-banks.

The other day I received from London a telegram saying that my books are already on their way to Berlin, without counting on Ugrimov[1] and Shishkin. I ask you to telegraph me when my baggage arrives: I will come immediately to Berlin myself.

If it arrives unexpectedly, and everything is done before my arrival , and my things are sent to you, then I would deem it a very great favor if you would put the books in your 'econom office', and take all the manuscripts and the typed documents (and there a lot of them) to store in your home, since among them there are very many of your documents.

Was my programme useful to you and did you receive (unreadable)? Did you find time to look over my writing; apropos – at the end of the chapter on capital, I have not described quite clearly the division of the budget into personal and farm expenditures (theory of labour-consumer balance). I am now correcting the ending.

I send warmest greetings and again thank you for sending me your package.

Greetings to E.D.

A. Chayanov

Lyolya sends her greetings!

NOTE

1.   Boris Ivanovich Ugrimov (1872–?), professor at the Superior Technical School, head of the Narkomzem Bureau for Electrification of Agriculture.

Letter 14

?December, 1922.   From Schreiberhau to Kuskova

Dear Ekaterina Dmitrievna!

When I received the Vologodskii collection,[1] I recognized your handwriting on the package and, inspired by gratitude, I thank you for this and for your many other concerns about us. We live covered with snow and in such ideal conditions as only can be imagined, and if we do not recover with phenomenal speed, it is only because we see absolutely no sunlight behind the plopping snow that falls 26 hours a day, which means that by night it falls with double hours.

With us for two days, visiting, were the Makarovs.[2] Nikolai Pavlovich and I succeeded in solving all the world's questions completely, and even a few problems of future centuries, which interested him, in the area of forecasting grain farming right up to the year 2400.

Very grateful for the gazette, even though I must admit that A.K. and his ilk have matured to such an extent that, after 36 'Days' one may again write 'Golos Rossii' freely. And, not disagreeably for the Eser, the heart problem of Kuskova, Peshekhonov and others has perceptibly lightened, and the health of the Eser corpse is newly restored and purified.[3]

We have great events daily, and also problems, because gradually, one after the other, garments are gathered by Lyolina and dispatched to you for safe-keeping, dresses destined for a minimum of 6 months to be unused.[4]

My economic work moves forward energetically and, by Christmas, everything except the introduction and conclusion will be ready.

For Christmas, we will have pastry and cakes, and even a Christmas tree, and if E.D. and S.N.[5] come by in the snow to visit for a few days and to rest from everything in Berlin, they will not be disappointed.

For this, at 10:15 you must sit down in the (train) coach at Görlitzer banhof and at 5 you will already be acquainted with the culinary arts of Frau De Ruyter.[6] Your furs will dry from the snow near the heat of the dutch stove. Barking will be the dog Ingo and arching its spine from happiness, the kitten 'Muxen' (both are Olgina's lovers). Sergei Nikolaevich will be convinced that the Rhein wine in Schreiberhau is no worse than in Berlin.

Truly! Come for Christmas.

Again greetings and thanks very much!

A. Chayanov

NOTES

1.   The Vologodskii collection contained the results of Prokopovich's farm-budget research in the vicinty of Vologda (Vologodskii Region), where, as it happened, he and Kuskova also spent part of their internal exile before their banishment from Russia. Chayanov had been asking Prokopovich for months to send him this material .

2.   Nikolai Pavlovich Makarov was one of Chayanov's closest colleagues in the Organization-Production School.. One of Chayanov's instructions from the Commissariat of Agriculture, when he left on his trip to western Europe, was to help the foreign ministry to facilitate the return to Moscow of Makarov, who had been abroad, mostly in the United States, for around three years at the time of this meeting in Schreiberhau. Makarov returned

to Moscow only in 1924.
3. 'A.K.' was Aleksandr Kerenskii, the brilliant but erratic Socialist Revolutionary leader, who was blamed by his Socialist Revolutionary rival, Viktor Chernov, for mistakes that led to the Bolshevik takeover. Both were part of Russian Berlin in the early 1920s. Chernov's colleagues controlled the newspaper *Golos Rossii* (*Russia's Voice*) until its demise in October 1922, whereupon Kerenskii's faction began publication of the newspaper *Dni* (*Days*), promising to carry on where *Golos Rossii* had left off. Chayanov's conclusion that 'A.K. and his ilk have matured' related to the 'gazette' that Kuskova had sent him, presumably issue number 36 of *Dni*. Kuskova, with her view favouring an end to armed opposition to the Bolsheviks, and her colleague, Aleksei Vasilevich Peshekhonov, a former leader of the Narodnii Socialist party who would later join the 'Changing Landmarks' movement, were natural targets for Kerenskii's scorn. It was Chayanov's assessment that their 'heart problem' had lightened with the 'purification' of the 'Eser corpse'. ('Eser' is an acronym for S.R. – Socialist Revolutionary.)
4. The reference is to Ol'ga's pregnancy, and the process of steadily out-growing her dresses.
5. Ekaterina Dmitrievna and Sergei Nikolaevich.
6. Frau De Ruyter, the proprietress of their mountain retreat.

Letter 15

2 January, 1923   From Mittelschreiber to Sokrat

Dear Sokrat!

Finding myself in Cologne, I was stunned by a wood engraving in two colors, ascribed to monographist A., working at the end of the XV century and portraying your ex libris. I made every effort and with the help of a Berlin antiquarian found another two reprints and proof sheets (probe blatt).

I am sending them to you for your collection and for exchange with collectors of book marks.

That is all on the subject of engravings. I will not send you anything more, since you do not answer my letters, with which my faithful wife sent you a wood engraving and other graphics that we very much fear were lost on the way to you.

The other day, I signed a contract with the publisher Paul Parey for publication in German of my new book on the peasant economy and I am now making the last corrections in the text that is already nearly finished and translated.

For the rest, we live well , as before, and when we get a letter from you Olgunka will write you about our latest engraving acquisitions.

I send you all thanks.

A. Chayanov

Happy New Year!

2 Jan. 1923. Mittelschreiber ... in Riesengebirge uberweg
    bei Frau prof Ruyter.

Letter 16

3. I.23 From Schrei berhau. To Prokopovich.

3.I.23 I wish you a Happy New Year!

Dear Sergei Nikolaevich!

I have just received your letter and I am answering by return post, first of all concerning your kind invitation to take a most active part in your journal,[1] the appearance of which I welcome in every way.

In itself, it is clear that, as far as having enough time, I could try to take an active part, but I think that publishing my name as an 'active participant' would hardly be helpful. I think the same applies to Makarov. From a formal point of view, the presence of Brutskus[2] testifies quite well to the representation of our positions, and I doubt that anyone will notice our absence, since my name and Makarov's are known only in very narrow circles and are mentioned very little by the general public. Tactically, we probably could be very helpful to you, but I don't want to create extra difficulties for my conversations with Lubyanka about my return to Moscow. It is evident that for you, me, Rykov, Teodorovich, taking part in the editing of an economic journal is not, in itself, criminal, but the ordinary Chekist distinguishes poorly between politics and economics.[3]

And, since Olgunka and I are thinking about returning to Moscow (X/23) at the first medical opportunity, then, unless there is a pressing necessity, there is no need for me to participate in a demonstration of joint work with P. Struve.[4]

To a still greater extent, I am pleased by your offer to to have me read through the course of 'Peasant Economy', which is especially valuable now, since nothing could be better for helping to finish my work than to read it, once more, with each other, to expound it orally in a pedagogical sense.

However, there are reasons, this time of a family nature, to do this during a quick visit in the form of a short encyclopedic course, since until March 1, Olgungkina's health requires us to remain in the mountains, and before April she and I hope to drop in, if only for two or three weeks, on Italy, I for the water economy, she to have a look at a never-before-seen antique culture.

If, for the scientific institute,[5] the technique of the Shanyanvskii University is applicable,[6] then in the course of February I can set forth in 3–4 lectures all the basic ideas and facts of the present doctrine of the peasant economy. If this variant, which is most convenient for me, does not work out we will arrange something different.

At the end of January, I must be in Berlin in order to complete our passports, and I can renew, and read through with you, the lectures. On the 'cooperative days', I don't wish to be present, since officially I now have no relationship with the cooperative institutions, have not received a formal invitation, and basically am not in agreement with them.[7]

I anticipate that on 13–14/I Makarov will be passing through Berlin. If you are interested in receiving a report from him, contact him immediately. He is in Geneva.

I read through your work, naturally, the very first evening that I received it. Methodologically, this is an outstandingly serious step forward. In general, Sergei Nikolaevich, as I think I have said to you, in the development of Russian economic thought, it has been your lot to be the pioneer of all of us in very many aspects of our science, and perhaps most of all with Western European scholars. Undoubtedly, the method of analytical coefficients of correlation will also have great significance beyond the borders of Russia, and I think that the best thing for you to do is to publish it in one of the English journals that specialize in the treatment of this question. In a few days, A.S. Orlov[8] will be in Berlin and probably will come to see you, and you can learn exactly how this is done, since he follows this literature closely, and is well-posted.

In the final analysis, what concerns me is that the theme seems insufficiently elaborated, and the receipt of profit provides very little for the theory. We are left, setting aside the rest to a series of additional questions and explanations from your side, with two observations:

1) A high coefficient of revenue from the sown area ... and so on, is clearly not very interesting, since it is technically related and all those elements, at bottom, are different expressions of one and the same occurrence – the size of the agricultural activity. Their theoretical value is the same as the value of a high coefficient of correlation between the number of sales of linen and the size of the monetary income of the Volokolamsk economy.

2) Your coefficients clarifying values of land provide very little for the appraisal of a specific gravity of the family, for the analysis is really not of farm income, but of the income of one worker. When we meet, I will inform you of all my doubts and questions. Until then, I send warmest greetings to you and E.D.

A. Ch.

Olgunka sends regards.

NOTES

1. Prokopovich's new journal was called Ekonomicheskii Vestnik (Economic Bulletin).
2. Ber Davidovich Brutskus (1878–1938). Economist and agronomist, initially identified with the agrarian policies of Stolypin. In a public discussion in Moscow at the height of the famine, Brutskus flatly declared that the famine was caused by the policy of the Soviet regime. Exiled in 1922.
3. The GPU (Secret Police), formerly called the CheKa, was headquartered in a large building on Lubyanskii Square in Moscow. The square, and later the building, came to be called Lubyanka. It also was the location of the dreaded 'inner prison'. The term 'Lubyanka' came to mean the bolsheviks' Secret Police, and the term 'Chekist' meant a Secret Policeman.
4. Petr Struve, a so-called 'legal' Marxist, had been a significant leader in socialist circles before the revolution, and had become a spokesman among emigrés in Berlin for conservative liberalism. It is probable that Prokopovich, who had much in common with Struve, envisioned some kind of joint activity involving Struve and Chayanov.
5. The reference is to Prokopovich's 'Economic Cabinet', which functioned in Berlin as a research institute on Russian subjects.
6. Prokopovich and Chayanov organised, before the war, at the 'people's' university in Moscow named for General Shanyavskii, a research center for the co-operative movement.
7. Although Chayanov did not explain his disaffection with the co-operative organisations, it coincided with a period of intense competition among participants in business and trade under the New Economic Policy, especially affecting the cooperatives and new, rival forms of enterprise.
8. A.S. Orlov (1871-1947), Academician who specialised in agricultural literature.

Letter 17

18. I. 23   From Berlin   To Yashchenko
Berlin. 18. I. 23

Dear Aleksandr Semenovich!

Makarov terrified me with his report about such a review that he did of the Kremnev utopia.

Since I do not at all wish to end up in Lubyanka on my return to Moscow, so again and again (I wrote to you about this already from England) I ask you to send me the review to censor. Makarov does not object. If the Number is already made-up – remove it from the make-up and substitute another.[1] Your portfolio already has enough.

In the most extreme case, I will land in the 'Hall of Columns' and all that publicity-political bravado.

In general, I would prefer that Moscow not be reminded about this work of mine, but inasmuch as the review is written, hold back the printing and dear God put in the corrections.

A. Chayanov.

Mittelschreiberhau in Riesengebirge
bei Frau Prof. De Ruyter
A. Tschayanoff

NOTE

1. The review by N. Makarov of Ivan Kremnev. *Puteshestvie moego brata Alekseya* – *NRK* 1922, No. 11–12. (appeared in January 1923).

ORIGINAL OF LETTER 17 IN CHAYANOV'S OWN HAND

Letter 18

?January, 1923   From Schreiberhau   To Sokrat

Dear Sokrat!

Regarding O.E.'s monograph on engravings, I think it is not out of place to raise several questions about the condition of the English and German markets for engravings. The offerings both here and there are very great and, if one has a lot of money, one can assemble a very nice collection in various fields, but all the same, first-class prints are scarce and extremely expensive, while there are many of second (class), and they are relatively reasonable.

The difference between prices in special shops, intended for American dilettantes, and small copper-plate 'kabinetami' are 3 or 4 times, but the richness of appearance, by the same token, is weaker.

In England there is everything, but especially many Hollander and black styles, while in Germany, naturally, a predominance of the old Germans.

English prices are well registered in catalogs and accounts of auctions and for one or another of the masters quite varied, depending on the place and state of preservation of the exemplars. I will quote a few, which should greatly interest you

£= pound st[erling]. S = shilling. d = penny. Bn No. 'po barchu'.
Schongaier[1] £6 – £200, Mantegna[2] £100 – £200 etc.
Hollanders Ostade[3] 'Oborvanets v plashche' / Bn 22/, 3, S 8,
'Prazdnik pod derevom' Bn 48 10, smaller for 1.
Rembrant[4] from £3 to £15, good and scarce sheets £100. 'List v 100 Guldenov',
Bad £25, good £1750.
Ruysdael[5] from £2 to £50.
Potter[6] £1–£3.
Waterloo, Bergam, Both for £1–£2, poorly printed S 5–10

Such heads (Takie golovi) as Lyolya sent you, for 2–3 shillings each, and at some bukinists just a shilling. On the other hand, let your heart be gladdened, Bartolozzi,[7] all around 5 and in the same price range many Pironezi.[8] Write the names of one or another and I will give you the exact information.

In Germany there are almost no Hollanders. Old Germans cost 4,000–25,000 marks (Kleinmeister[9]) Krannax,[10] Baldung Grin[11] and Durer[12] 25–150 thousand. Wood engravings, cut from books of the XVI century, 500–1,000 marks, all this at an exchange rate of £1 = 32,000 marks.

A great number of masters of the XVIII century and XIX century for 100–200 marks; prime pieces are very costly and are sold for pounds at London prices.

For our modest means, it behooves us to be content with small and unimportant prints. In general, our purchases in London fluctuated from 1 to 4 shillings for Hollanders , and from S 5 to S 15 for old Germans. In Germany we pay from 300 marks to 10,000 each and altogether, buying very prudently, we have 35 old Germans, 15 Hollanders, 10 Italians and around 20 various others, all more or less satisfactory. Besides which we were purchasers of 3–4 prime pieces of the highest museum character, including 1 Aldegreber,[13] 2 Begam,[14] 1 Durer, Kallo[15] and Ostaus.[16]

However, I must admit the fact that the quality of our purchases of sheets surely would permit us to sell them at auction for 2–3 times higher than the purchase price.

I very much ask you to tell us whether you received the 2 volumes of mystery books, sent to you by Zherebtsov, and (kineta) 7 wooden portraits of the XVI century. Until later.

A.

Enclosed I send 2 (holzschnitt'a [wood engravings], which O.E. sends for your collection and asks you to determine the school and time and write them to her.

A.Ch.

NOTES

1. Martin Schongauer (1450–91), German painter/engraver.
2. Andre Mantegna (1431–1506), Italian painter.
3. Adriaen van Ostade (1616–85), Dutch artist, student of Frans Hals.
4. Rembrandt Harmenszood van Rijn (1606–69), Dutch painter and etcher.
5. Jacob Ruysdael (1629–82), Dutch paysagiste.
6. Paulus Potter (1625–54), Dutch paysagiste.
7. Francesco Bartalozzi (1727–1815), Florentine artist.
8. Giovanni Batista Piranesi (1720–78), Venetian artist.
9. Kleinmeister, also known as 'Die Nurnberger Kleinmeister', a group of engravers influenced by Albrecht Durer, working mostly in Nurnberg in the 16th century, producing small, easily portable engravings.
10. Lucas Cranach (1472–1553), German engraver.
11. Hans Baldung (Grun) (1480–1545), Alsatian painter and engraver.
12. Albrecht Durer (1471–1528), German painter and engraver, born in Nurnberg,
13. Heinrich Aldegrever (1502–60), engraver and jeweller.
14. Hans Sebald Beham (1500–50) [Begam], the most prolific of the 'Kleinmeister'.
15. Jacques Callot (1592–1635) French painter and engraver.
16. 'Ostaus' (probably is a transliteration error of the handwritten entry '"Ostade"' (see Adriaen van Ostade in Note 3 above).

Letter 19

? February, 1923   From Schreiberhau   To Sokrat

Dear Sokrat!

I am very happy that the witch-doctor is curing you of your illness and I am even a little ashamed that I was so angry with you for your stubborn postal silence ... I am counting on receiving from you in the nearest time a compensatorily long epistle, and then I must ask you for an explanation of what is, to me, a very strange and odd incident ... From a letter of E.V.[1] I learn with amazement that she has received, through you and Galya,[2] a Christmas present and money, allegedly from me. Inasmuch as I sent nothing, neither to you, nor, even more, to Galia, about sojourns which in Moscow were not even suspected, then naturally I was cast in a most painful bewilderment.

What is it all about? Why did you find it necessary to cloak an obviously personal gift with my name, placing me in the foolish situation of receiving unworthy thanks and creating still greater complications ... I do not know anything at this moment about the material situation of E.V. Perhaps her friends had to take this action, but why in such a form?

I ask you urgently to write about what's happening – because an explanation is extremely necessary for me.

So much for these unpleasant events, now I turn to you, personally. I am trying very hard to find out from Fridrikhson about your invitation to Berlin and your assignment to him, and until now have not been successful, but I am also trying to persuade Osinskii about this, since he has been living here for about three months. In any case, I hope it has not been forgotten, and will pursue this matter. Perhaps you yourself can take some steps in this respect. You do not necessarily need a lot of money to live in Germany, and I may be able, in the course of a month, to finance some simple economic work for you. At this time, I am publishing my fat book in the German language with Paul Parey, and have already published two of my articles in the 'Archiv f. soc. W i. Socpolit' and 'Schmollers Jahrbuch'.

I am beginning work on the water economy and , in my free time, I am discussing with Ol'ga the study of engraving, about which she is writing to you herself.

Did you receive my 'exlibrises' and how did they strike you? Write for me the titles of your best Piranesi and Bartalozzi and I will send you the London valuation. Then I will send you two ordinary engraved enclosures, of which one is especially interesting. Apropos, in your collection there is an etching of mine with a pair of cupids. I have seen exactly such a sheet and it appears to belong to the Bolognese master Lorenzo Lolli (1612–90), a student of Guido Reni, price 6/-.

Well then, farewell and do not forget to write to me quickly explaining about the Christmas gift, and if you can not do it because of your illness, ask Galya, from whom in any case I have not received a letter.

Your A. Chayanov

P.S. Ask Iv. Iv. Lazarevskii[3] why he does not print my article on Moscow collectors of the beginning of the XIX century. So let Moscow not print it. Moscow is full of mistakes.

Hurry with your answer, because without clarification from you I do not know what to reply to E.V.

NOTES

1. Elena Vasilevna Grigoreva, Chayanov's first wife.
2. Galya Klepikova, Sokrat's wife.
3. Ivan Ivanovich Lazarevskii, Editor of the journal *Sredi Kollektsionerov/Among Collectors*. Chayanov contributed articles to Lazarevskii's journal.

Letter 20

? Feb./March 1923   From Schreiberhau to Sokrat

My dear Sokrat!

Just now I have received the letter from Mikh(ail]. Evgenevich, <u>partly</u> explaining 'my' Christmas present. But you yourself understand that such an explanation, in this case, is a half-explanation, and if the material situation of Elena Vasilievna is such that she required help of such extravagant means, then would it not have been better to write directly to me about this? Therefore, I urgently ask you to respond to me <u>exactly</u>:

1. Does E.V. need permanent material help, or was her Christmas without money merely by chance?

2. Why has A.A.[1] allowed such a crisis, in spite of his guarantee that he gave to me before I left?

Life's path for Elena Vasilievna and me is finished, forever, but I can not tolerate a situation in which a person who lived one life with me for nine years would experience need at a time when I was in a position to help her.

Therefore, until I have your answer, I am sending (mail) for Degtyarnyi [ARCh][2] and await your letter, with a fundamental explanation of this whole question. I want to make it clear that, neither about this letter nor about your reply, must E.V. know anything.

Now it is time for material questions, and Olya and I have decided, after studying all the Moscow letters, to ask you directly whether you need money for your treatment, and for your cost of living in a time of forced unemployment, and so I ask only about how much, since it is entirely clear that you are, in fact, in need, given that you have already spent three months lying in bed.

I think of you as the closest person to me from the male half of our human ancestry, and therefore my sympathy is not an insult, but just an expression of my brotherly feelings toward you.

Our situation here is not especially scintillating, but when it comes to helping you, I feel I can freely do it, and you must understand, that in your time of need I would come running to help you, just as you came running in a most critical moment of my life.[3]

And therefore I am not compelled to apply to you your method, that you displayed in relation to E.V.

So that is it for now! Give us an answer quickly.

We are healthy and courageous, insofar as it is possible to be courageous in a country trembling on the foundation of its destiny.[4] Maybe it will turn out that in a month we will already be in Italy.

Warmly shake your hand.

A. Chayanov

I am sending you an engraving by Hans Sebald Beham from the collection 'Free Art'.

P.S. I am making every effort to drag you here to be cured, but just now it is not entirely clear to me what the motives in Moscow are and I don't know exactly where to turn. The easiest of all, for me, would of course be NKZ, but I do not know about your current relationship with them, and Narkompros[5] I think is hopeless. I think that the very best would be if you were simply free to cure your illness, since in any case, to begin with, there is nothing you can do here. Find out the address of Mimotin and Lomov[6] and write me; they are morally obliged to help you to recover, and I will write to them.

NOTES

1. Aleksei Aleksandrovich Rybnikov. artist and illustrator, did the illustrations for one of Chayanov's romantic tales, later married Chayanov's first wife, Elena Vasilievna. (Not to be confused with Aleksandr Aleksandrovich Rybnikov, one of Chayanov's closest friends and collaborators in the Organization-Production school.)
2. This suggests that Chayanov was sending mail on this subject to someone other than his ex-wife.
3. The reference may be to the dark period when Chayanov's first wife left him for Alexei Rybnikov.
4. Potriasennoi do osnovaniia sudboi.
5. Narkompros: People's Commissariat of Enlightenment. The Commissar was Anatoly Lunacharskii.
6. G. I. Lomov (Oppokov) (1888–1937), worked in party and economic bureaux.

Letter 21

? February   From Schreiberhau   To Sokrat

Dear Sokrat!

Huge thanks to you for your two letters written from your sick-bed. According to your instructions, I have (1) written to London so that in two or three days (unreadable) will be sent to A.R.; (2) sent a letter that El. Vas.[1] may use, addressed to the Collegium of N.K.Z., for Kamenev[2] and for Sadyrin[3] on the matter of a contract for the house. It is necessary to settle with Sadyrin's lawyer and get from Kard< ... > a paper from the collegium of N.K.Z., saying that I can not come in person and that the contract must be signed by E.V., at the request of the collegium. Her letter to Kamenev should be used only in case of emergency, since I have already negotiated through Petrovka, with the communal department, to arrange our moving into an apartment, and I fear that too great a clamor about Degtyarnii might put me in a hopeless situation in the fall, when I return to Moscow with Ol'ga, mama and our new-born child, who is arriving in May.

It seems to me that my message is sufficient for the renewal of the contract, in which case Vas. Nik., through Mikhailovskii[4] in the communal department, can do more, I think, than I, and also Aleksei Rybnikov with all his shiftiness may protect and rescue E.V. in any case. If my letter is insufficient, send a telegram and I will endeavor, through the local representative, to help telegraphically.

Now, to work. Thank you very much for your intention to send *Among Collectors*. I have numbers 9 and 10, and they are for sale everywhere in Berlin. I will be very thankful if you will send my books *History of Budget Research* TsSU[5] and 'Collection of Articles', that already long ago should have come to N.K.Z. (here) (according to a telephone report of M. Ya. Belenka).

Then, I ask you to answer precisely, did you receive two volumes of Olcott,[6] the mystery books, sent by me to your account when I was still in London, and three copies of ex libris for your library work as monographist.

I don't have any confirmation from you about them and would very much like to know whether they were sent on to you. In any case I enclose (in despair of proof, unfortunately), another ex libris.

Would be extremely grateful if you could undertake two engraving commissions:

1) Sending for one week, with a guarantee of return, a catalog of the exhibition in the Rum. M.[7] 'Epochs of Engraving'.

2) Sending an exhaustive list of literature about engraving.

In exchange, I will send you a remingtonned copy of my instruction for collecting western engravings. If one has German money, just now, one can gather a whole cabinet of engravings. My cheap purchases sometimes bring us beautiful sheets. Thus, traveling through Dresden, I succeeded in buying a sheet IB and a sheet Sprienkenklee.

My economic work follows its usual course, and I must think that, in the fall , I will return with not one, but three books, yes, + 'Old Engravings' (ask Lazarevskii if he won't agree to publish them), 3 printed sheets without illustrations.

Large greetings to you from Olgunka.

A. Chayanov

My address beginning 3 March

Heidelberg, Rohrbacherstr 80 bei Frau E.V.Wining.

NOTES

1. Elena Vasilievna, Chayanov's former wife. Before the break-up of their marriage, they had lived on Degtyarnyi Lane in the heart of Moscow. In the early 1920s, housing became extremely scarce and harsh restrictions were placed on the square footage residents were allowed to have. Chayanov sought to settle his ex-wife and her new husbcand, Alexei Rybnikov, in the Degtyarnyi house, assuming that he would receive living space at the Petrovkii (Timiryazevskyi) Agricultural Academy.
2. Lev Kamenev (Rosenfeld) was deputy chairman of the Soviet government, and also chairman of the Moscow soviet. He had been chairman of the All-Russian Famine Committee of which Chayanov was a member,
3. Pavel Alekseevich Sadyrin was an agricultural scientist, like Chayanov, and held leadership positions in organizations of agricultural cooperatives.
4. Nikolai Konstantinovich Mikhailovskii, writer and literary critic, said to have played a role in shaping Chayanov's world outlook. Apparently, he held a position in the Moscow agency that controlled the assignment of living space.
5. Tsentralnogo Statisticheskogo Upravleniia (Central Statistical Administration)
6. Henry Steele Olcott, with his wife, Elena Petrovna Blavatskaia, founded the Theosophical Society. Author of a Bulddhist Catechism. Authority on occultism.
7. Rumantsev Museum.

Letter 22

2 March, 1923   From Schreiberhau   To Sokrat

Dear Sokrat!

I am writing you my last letter from Schreiberhau. Tomorrow morning we leave for Heidelberg and expect to be there until our return to Moscow. Our address, as I already told you, is Heidelberg, Rohrbacherstr. 80, bei Frau E.V. Winning.

I ask you very seriously not to reject my request, and to compile copies of all books known to you about engraving in the Russian language, and then to report what you know about Russian engravings before Peter and separately in the XVIII century, briefly.

I have almost finished my book on old engravings, needing only to write the chapters 'Engraving in France' and 'Engraving in Russia', and a few other things very briefly for 3–4 pages, since my center is in the XV, XVI and XVII centuries.

Regards to Galya and everyone. A. Chayanov

N.N. Enclosing, this time, the following: Antonio Tempesta (1555–1630),[1] Bartsch,[2] 125 m. XVII.

NOTES

1.   Florentine artist.
2.   Adam von Bartsch (1757–1821), Austrian artist.

Letter 23

13 III 23. Berlin.

ИСТОРІА ПАРИКМАКЕРСКОЙ КУКЛЫ

ИЛИ

Последная любовь Московскаго архитектора М.

Дорогому тезке и
рецензенту от признательный
автора
*   13 III 23 А. Чаянов*
Berlin

STORY OF THE HAIRDRESSER'S MANNEQUIN

or

The Last love of the Moscow architect M.

To Dear Namesake and
Critic from
the grateful author
*   13 III 23 A. Chaianov*
Berlin

ORIGINAL OF LETTER 23 IN CHAYANOV'S OWN HAND

ИСТОРІЯ ПАРИКМАХЕРСКОЙ КУКЛЫ

или

Послѣдняя любовь Московскаго архитектора М.

ИЗДАНИЕ АВТОРА.

Р. В. Ц. г. Сергиев 1921 г.   Тираж 1.000.

Типография при Отд. Нар. Образования Серг. Совета.

Letter 24

14.III.23   Berlin

ОБМАНЩИКИ

ТРАГЕДИЯ

Дорогому тезке
и милому критику
снисходительному от
автора с глубокой
благодарностью

А. Чаянов
Берлин
     14 III 23

THE CHEATERS

TRAGEDY

To Dear namesake
and charming indulgent
critic from
the author with deepest
gratitude.

     A. Chaianov.
     Berlin
       14 III 23

ORIGINAL OF LETTER 24 IN CHAYANOV'S OWN HAND

Letter 25

?March 1923   From Heidelberg   To Kuskova

Dear Ekaterina Dmitrievna!

First of all, deep thanks from mama ... The closer we come to the moment of the appearance in the world of our child, the more helpless I feel, and the more important the arrival of mama becomes. Thanks to your exceptional kindness and your efforts, I now hope to succeed in arranging mama's arrival before the appearance of the little one, something about which I was beginning to doubt ... Once again great thanks for your kindness and sympathy.

Mama's address: Moscow, Povarskaya, Xlebnii lane 9, Apt. 4. (Elena Konstantinovna Chayanova, maiden name Klepikova, born 4 March 1863 in Vyatski gub.)

We are slowly, but surely, acclimatizing ourselves , and in every way we already are registered as Heidelberg dwellers.

Once again, great thanks.

A. Chayanov.

Letter 26

18.IV.1923   From Heidelberg   To Prokopovich
Honorable Sergei Nikolaevich!

The book of Chernenkov[1] is not to be found on my shelves in Heidelberg, and since it certainly was sent to me, then it either was mislaid during the packing at [?...Hilm'y ..)[2] or perhaps is still at your place on a shelf of books that I left in your office.

As far as I remember, I asked Ol'ga to write to Ekaterina Dmitrievna about this in a letter, in which she wrote about the arrival of mama at your house. It's very embarrassing, that inadvertently it resulted from carelessness.

Concerning the Epifanskii district, Vikhlyayeva in Moscow also wrote about it, but there is no answer and there may not be. In the same way there is no answer from Moscow about the publication of your book, about which Ekaterina Dmitrievna spoke to me when X was in Berlin.

The other day, I finished 'To the question of an economic theory of a non-capitalist system of national economy'. It came to 2 pages of compressed text. I will let it mature, and then have it published in the 'Archiv fur .SW und .SP', whose editorial office, with which I often have close contact, happens to be in Heidelberg. On economic policy, I still cannot seriously concentrate – I work by fits and starts. Evidently, I am still not mature.

Greetings to Ekaterina Dmitrievna!
A. Chayanov.
18.IY.23
I am sending your Village and Local Economy.

NOTES

1. Nikolai Nikolaevich Chernenkov (1863–?).
2. The reference indicates that the Pension 'Hilma', where the Chayanovs stayed when they arrived in Berlin, may have been used as a transfer point when his baggage was shipped from London.

Letter 27

?April,1923   From Heidelberg   To Baxrax.

I enclose the final version of the tale that I read to you, concerning which I make the following request. If it is not too much trouble, then ask Vishnyak[1] if he would not like to publish it in Helikon, using the new format, and not as part of a collection but as a separate publication. It is very necessary to have these conditions – the new orthography and a 2 or 3-month deadline for publication. As an honorarium, I would be pleased to have 50 copies. The right of second publication I retain for myself. If Vishnyak is not interested himself, and none of the other printing houses is interested in publishing it, then I would like to publish it at my own expense, but I do not know how this is done, technically.[2]

NOTES

1. Abram Grigorievich Vishnyak was the editor of Helikon publishing house, first in Moscow, then in Berlin.
2. The book was published by Helikon, at Chayanov's expense.

Letter 28

? May, 1923   From Heidelberg   To Sokrat

Sokrat! Enclosing Hand Kolorierte Holzschnitt which has the purpose of informing you that to us on I V 23 was born a son, Nikita.

And besides this, a request, and a very important one – when I departed, I left, and if my memory does not deceive me, left in your name – my articles on Moscow collectors of the XVIII and XIX centuries for *Among Collectors*. For a whole year I have been scolding Lazarevskii because he has not printed it and now I remember that they were never delivered to him. If you have not lost them, then remember where they are and quickly go ... But if they have been collected and already are lost, then somewhere at Degtyarnii[1] there must be second copies. I urgently ask you to search for them, and deliver them to the editorial office.

Greetings,
A. Chayanov.
Heidelberg, Rohrbacherst. 80

NOTE

1.   This reference to Degtyarnii Lane indicates that Chayanov may have been living there until his departure in 1922.

Letter 29

? May, 1923   From Heidelberg   To Baxrax.

Deepest thanks to you for your efforts. Judging from your letter, all is going splendidly. The hardest thing of all is to transfer money in hard currency from Heidelberg.[1]

Perhaps Vishnyak knows a method of transferring money in pounds? The hard currency is already waiting in an envelope[2] – and is at your disposal. I regret that you are only preparing to come to us in Heidelberg, but have not actually come. It is not very far at all, altogether only one night.

NOTES

1. This was Germany in the period of inflation, when the slightest delay in the transfer of the German mark led to its complete depreciation.
2. Eleven English pounds ('but in those days this amount for people living in Germany amounted to capital' – Baxrax).

Letter 30

8 May, 1923.   From Heidelberg   To Baxrax

Be so good as to write me frankly – is it really worth publishing this tale of the *Venetian Mirror*, or would it be better to incorporate it into the portfolio of my unpublishable manuscripts? It seems to me, personally, that the *Mirror* has been rather exhausted by numerous alterations, and to work on it any further – I just cannot, since I have completely gone out of the circle of its psychology. To you as the first of my critics I leave the final word. If you think that it holds up for publication, then we also must think about an artist, since I want to do, as I did with Venediktov, a book jacket, frontispiece [as in the original] and a tail-piece. One thing more, the book should be published in a month's time – is this possible? In Moscow I could produce it in 4 days.[1]

And now, since I still have a little time left from my scientific work, I am writing a 'big novel' – 'The Extraordinary but True adventure of F. Mix. Buturlin' – (18th century in Moscow), which satisfies me more than did, in their time, all the other tales.

NOTE

1.   Illustrations for the book were not arranged.

Letter 31

22 May.   From Heidelberg   To Baxrax.

Buturlin all written, and I am mailing you a fair copy.

Letter 32[1]

2 June, 1923   From Heidelberg   To Baxrax.

(a) On the morning of the 10th of June I will arrive in Berlin on the Munich train and on the same day I would like to visit you. . .

(b) By the way, I am bringing with me a completely finished "Buturlin", and if, in the course of the 10th, 11th and until 7 in the evening of the 12th, you and Rax Gri[2] find the time and the desire to listen for 1.5 hours to a stunning fantasy, I would with great pleasure read it to you and to any others whom you find it useful to invite for this reading.

NOTES

1. This letter represents excerpts from Baxrax and Chertkov [*Baxrax*, 1982].
2. Rakhila Grigorevna Osorgina, wife of novelist and felllow member of the anti-hunger committee, Mikhail Osorgin.

Letter 33

?June 15, 1923   From Heidelberg   To Narkomzem.

(From Nikonov [1989]
Biographical material by A.A. Nikonov)

NOTE: The full texts of the letters excerpted here were not available. A portion of Professor Nikonov's commentary is presented to provide the contexts of the excerpts.

[Page 16] ... 'In the summer of 1923, they lived in the little German town of Heidelberg, that was situated between Frankfurt-on-Main and Stuttgart, not far from Mannheim. From there, in June, he literally bombarded Narkomzem and economist-agrarians with letters with really interesting proposals. The matter was that Western economists, Germans above all (professor Zering), were working on a grandiose project: The status of world agriculture and trade in agricultural products after the war. Taking part also were Russian scientists, and the authors' collective was formed by A.V.Chayanov.   As the responsible editor of the Russian section, he persuaded to take part N.P. Makarov, N.P. Oganovskii, A.N. Chelintsev, A.I. Khryaschev, B.N. Knipovich, G.A. Studenskii, A.E. Losintskii, N.D. Kondrat'ev, I.M. Zhirkovich, P.I. Lyashchenko and others from Narkomzem.'

'On 15 June Chayanov wrote a letter to Narkomzem colleagues saying he was attending to the assignment from his colleagues at Narkomzem with extreme diligence. And here he displayed his really marvelous composure, self-control, in the final analysis, his know-how in trading.

He wrote: "Purchasing is complicated by the necessity for the most careful selection of books and by waiting for the best time of competition on the market. Purchasing books is done most cheaply at the time of a decline in the rate of exchange of the Mark."'

Later, he wrote ... 'Buying continues ... includes a range of foreign scholars: Germans, English and Russian.'

Note: The Central Agricultural library shows that from 1923–25 around 4,000 books of foreign scholars were acquired.)

Letter 34

?June, 1923   From Heidelberg   To Studenskii

Dear Gennadii![1]

In all probability, the composition of your work for Professor Sering[2] is drawing to a close. I urgently ask you to send it to me, not by simple post, which in recent times has become not very punctual, but through the collegium of NKZem and Krestinsky[3] in Berlin, with a dip-courier.[4]

Inform me on the status of the work on the egg market, and likewise the articles ordered from Kondrat'ev, Oganovskii and Lositskii, and whether at last their composition will be finished.

Further, I urgently need to know the status of publication for 'Ocherkov po Teorii Trudovogo Khozyaistva' ('Outline for a Theory of Working Farms') in *Novoi Derevne (The New Village)*[5] and if it still hasn't been published, then why?

For me all is as before, felicitous. Our son conducts himself magnificently and does not interfere with my work. I am working now on a theory of the price of slaves and serfs for the fall number of *Arkhiv fur Socialwissenschaft und Socialpolitik.*[6]

Regards to all.

A. Chayanov.

NOTES

1. Gennadii Aleksandrovich Studenskii (1892–1930). Agrarian Economist, close friend and colleague of Chayanov at the Petrovskii Academy and in Chayanov's Research Institute. Committed suicide after his imprisonment in 1930.
2. Profesor Max Sering (Zering), a prominent German agronomist.
3. Nikolai Nikolaevich Krestinsky, Soviet ambassador to Germany.
4. Diplomatic courier
5. One chapter of a work entitled 'Ocherki po Ekonomike Trudovogo Selskogo Khazyaistva' ('Outline for the Economy of Working Farms') was published in the journal *Sel. i Les. Khozyaistva (Agricultural and Forest Economies)* for May–June, 1923, in Moscow. The book was published in 1924, with an introduction by Lev Kritsman, a leader of the Agrarian Marxists.
6. The 'price of slaves and serfs' was an element in his work on non-capitalist economies.

Letter 35

?July, 1923. From Heidelberg. To Prokopovich

PETROVSKAJA LANDWIRTSCHAFTLICHE AKADEMIE
(MOSKAU)
WISSENSCHAFTLICHES FORSCHUNGSINSTITUT
FÜR AGRARÖKONOMIE UND AGRARPOLITIK

. . . .
MOSKAU, ARBAT, BOLSCHOJ-NIKOLOPESKOWSKIJ, 9

Dear Sergei Nikolaevich!

I direct to you, herewith, the blame for your discontent with me, which finally appears in its full light. [Posylaia], I have examined one more time all the formulations and I still do not entirely understand your discontentment, since theoretically this is a logical development of the old positions of Gessen, Jevons,[1] and, in its empirical part, it is more prudent , which hardly can be denied.

If I am utilizing the method of correlation in a minor fashion, it is your fault, since you have not, up to now, published the full results of your research. I have no desire to present myself as someone performing work parallel to yours.

Would be very happy if you would come to see us in Heidelberg along with Ekaterina Dmitrievna, who has arranged to be with us some time in September. On my return to Moscow, I plan to assemble a very large aggregation of scientific work and would like to have your guidance.

Deep greetings to Ekaterina Dmitrievna.

A.Ch.   (prof. A.V. Chayanov)

NOTE

1. William Stanley Jevons (1835–82) discussed the concept of a balance between 'need'and 'labour' in *The Theory of Political Economy*, London, 1911. Sergei Iosifovich Gessen (1887–1950) was a philosopher, pedagogue and political theorist.

Letter 36

? July, 1923   From Heidelberg   To Kuskova

Dear Ekaterina Dmitrievna!

I want very much to thank you for your lovely letter and telegram, and to express my utmost regret that evidently we just will not see you in Heidelberg; and since Ol'ga will be going to Moscow in a direct wagon Cologne-Riga, you thus, in general, deprive Ol'ga of the possibility of showing you her son.

At the same time, I must point out to you some inconsistencies. You write that it will be difficult to undergo treatment at a summer kurort near Berlin unless you abandon – because of the conflict of time – the idea of spending the summer in Baden Baden (which is almost next to us), and yet, at the same time, also go to Prague.[1] Any serious political commotion at this time would be like poison for you.

I very much admire the civil courage with which you recently defended your positions, and I want in every way to wish you strength in dealing with the difficult, and sometimes base (Yablonovskii),[2] accusations against you.

But at the same time, speaking frankly, I think that all the loquacious emigré pseudo-politicians taken together are not worth 1/10 the value of your health.

It could be that your struggle would bring only a Pyrrhic victory. You are not to blame that Messrs. Yablonovskii in their time could not get passing grades in even a preparatory class in political literacy, but trying to teach them now would surely be like hitting your head against a brick wall.

So perhaps it would not be all that disagreeable just now to abandon the journalists, and come by train to Heidelberg, if only for a week, and then go on to Baden Baden for 2 or 3 months. I guarantee that, in the end, you will be satisfied. Here with us, you will find everything in bloom, and although the French are only 15 versts (9 miles) away,[3] nevertheless we exist, as if in your blessed 80s.

Yesterday Rikert refutes all naturalism, today Saxo-Borussia (a corporation) organizes a torchlight procession (Fackelzug), and tomorrow an auction of household things by a middle class women's association, but such a cinema!!!, such a Rhein wine! If S.N. knew one and the other, he would carry you off by main force and bring you to Heidelberg.

So – we wait!

My most ardent greetings to Evgenii Ivanovna!

We send greetings.

All the best.

A.Ch.

NOTES

1. Berlin, at this time, was no longer the inexpensive paradise for foreigners that it had been. An exodus was beginning. Kuskova and Prokopovich were undoubtedly investigating the possibility of moving to Prague. Toward the end of the year, they did just that.

2. Aleksandr Yablonovskii was a contributor to the right-wing Kadet newspaper Rul', and a fierce polemicist who attacked everyone, including Kuskova, who appeared to be 'soft' on Bolshevism. Kuskova was neither a 'Eurasianist' nor a proponent of 'Changing Landmarks', but she proposed to 'fill in the trenches of the civil war' as a necessary precondition for a viable Russian society.
3. Heidelberg was just barely outside the zone in the Rhineland that the French had occupied in January, 1923, installing an exceedingly harsh rule that made life miserable for everyone living in the zone.

Letter 37

10 Aug. 1923.   From Heidelberg   To Prokopovich

Dear Sergei Nikolaevich!

It made me very sad to receive your letter in such a critical and cold form. The lines in my article[1] which are devoted to communism, or more precisely to governmental collectivism, occupy an insignificant place in the piece, and I would really like to know your thinking on its central part – the analysis of the slave and serf economy.[2] Is this not also possible with your 'Eurasia'?[3]

Further, when I include communism in a general table,[4] merely as a conceivable system, I am including a natural construction, one which many of my German correspondents are inclined to consider quite acceptable in an economic theory. It is in this connection that I propose for your two-fold consideration: a Communist national economic system turns out to be altogether acceptable within the general category of a national economy, and at the same time you are right, in your well-known judgment that it 'negates economy', in the sense that one judges an ideal, traditional economy. All this considered, I nevertheless, while completely unconcerned about the question of its practicability, was right to have touched on it as a proper, very strong current of agronomic thought, peculiar to Russian society.

Now, two words on what is most important – I am struck by several lines in your review of the book of Litoshenko.[5]

Only in my immature work, only in the books of Sherbina[6] and even much earlier budgetary research, did I calculate that 'The minimum living wage of the peasant is a constant quantity' etc. Already in my 'Outline of a theory of the working farm' in edition I, where, as you quite correctly point out, my theory was formulated, I theoretically (#4, beginning of page 10) came to a conclusion on the variability of growth of consumption, and only under the constraint of the very small amount of completely empirical material that I had then, was compelled, contrary to my theory, to use a fixed growth of consumption and to accept a theoretical correction, suggested to me by V.K. Dmitriev,[7] who then was my only leader in my work, and whom you hardly can accuse of 'Evraziistve' ('Eurasianism').

These theoretical corrections (compared to the development of the function CD)[8] were obvious quibbles and, as I recall, with the second edition of my 'Outline for a theory of the working farm' in 1913, I stood on the plane of recognition of the changeability of the growth of prosperity, something that was especially clear already in the Starobelskoi work, or to put it another way, returning to the simple (without Dmitriev's correction) theory of the work-consumption balance.

In short, I confirm that the theory of a work-consumption balance is incompatible with the idea of a fixed growth of consumption, as it is equally incompatible with the natural order of the economy, which, as Manuilov[9] and Litoshenko confirm, I apply to the basic doctrine.

Besides this, dear Sergei Nikolaevich, in order to avoid misunderstanding later, from the moment of the appearance of my Principles of a Peasant Economy,[10] I have been subjected to criticism of the formulation of the theory, established in chapter IV of the book (as will be pointed out in the introduction to the Russian edition), since just there is where the question is raised for the first time in all its complexity. In many immature and youthful works of mine, the calculation of capital restoration and the general role of capital in the working farm was completely neglected. It would help you tremendously to spend an hour and read through chapters IV and III of my book.

In conclusion I must say that in the theory we developed on the analysis of the materials of over-populated regions, and in our youthful work, many cases that appeared to be individual examples, peculiar to the north black earth and linen regions, began to be seen as general cases.

In the present condition of the theory on this subject I have found a specific gravity, and the theory is free of these errors.

In general, it seems to me that if you can find it acceptable to recognize a theory of peasant farming without the idea of wages and the simple profit of capitalist thought, then all disagreements between us are easily removed and one evening is enough, closely spent in discussion, in order for them to disappear.

Indeed your charges against me of Eurasianism, Sergei Nikolaevich, are founded not on my theory of the working farm, but on assumptions you have made based on political conclusions you have drawn from this theory. 'Assumptions': because I never, and to no one, ever formulated them.

Here perhaps agreement will be difficult, but all the same, I suppose that even here we will find several points of common interest if, of course, we exclude present day problems, in relation to which we conceive even the facts differently.

Deep thanks for the book.

A.Ch.   10 august 1923

NOTES

1. Chayanov's article 'To the Question of Economic Theory in a Non-Capitalistic System of National Economy'. (See Letter 24).
2. In his article, Chayanov devoted much space to analysis of a 'Slave Economy' and a 'Quitrent Serf Economy'. Chayanov had sent his manuscript to Prokopovich.
3. In Berlin, at this time, "Eurasianism", the concept that Russian civilisation was neither European nor Asian, but a melding of the two influences into a third entity, had become a hotly-disputed political movement, tending to promote toleration of the Bolshevik regime as the only viable guarantor of Russian power.
4. In his article, Chayanov established a table comparing the attributes of 8 economic systems: Capitalism, Commodity Economy, Natural Economy, Slave Economy, Quitrent Serf Economy, Landlord Economy, Peasant Economy, Communism.
5. Lev Nikolaevich Litoshenko (1886–1936). Economist, professor at Timiryazevskii Academy. Opposed the concept of consumption as a force in Russian agriculture, favored the concept of acquisitiveness. In the 1925 edition of his book, Chayanov responded to Litoshenko's criticism.
6. Fedor Andreevich Shcherbina (1849–1936), Agrarian scientist, pioneer in research dealing with farm budgets.
7. Vladimir Karpovich Dmitriev (1868–1913), economist, mathematician, statistician.
8. The function CD refers to Chayanov's graphical demonstration of his theory that the degree of self-exploitation of labour on a family farm is established by a relationship between the measure of demand satisfaction and the measure of the drudgery of the labor. In his graph, he generates two intersecting curved lines, A–B and C–D. The curve A–B represents the degree of drudgery and the curve C–D represents the marginal utility of the labour, measured in roubles. Where the two curves cross is where the farmer stops working because the ruble he earns is not worth the drudgery of earning it.

9. Aleksandr Apollonovich Manuilov (1861–1929). Minister of Enlightenment in the Provisional government in 1917. After the Bolshevik revolution, emigrated, but returned to work with the Bolshevik regime.
10. This book was published, with the help of Prokopovich, in Berlin in 1923, and translated into German by Dr Friedrich Schlömer. At the time of this letter, Prokopovich had had time to read it.

Letter 38

July/August, 1923   From Heidelberg   To Kuskova

(Letter without a salutation.)

[x x x missing text x x x] the West and a place in a cemetery.

If indeed it is our thought to remain with Russia (and I hope more than anything for exactly this), then we must fit ourselves into this thought.

But here the question is – how to fit in, and into what do we fit, and this is a hard task to resolve. On a small scale, perhaps, it can be done. Thus it is that I understand our publicist work. It is necessary, firmly and with determination, to separate Russia and the USSR. It is necessary to recognize the true process in the national economy, even to cooperate with this process, the intelligentsia, working with the Soviet regime. If we don't do this, we will become trash, and remain forever on Russia's sideline. Our writings will be mere bags of wind. Nowhere, and by nobody will we be believed. We need objectivity. with which to reveal ever more clearly the obstacles, created by the Soviet regime, to the development of the national economy, and that is what we should do as soon as possible.

For the realisation of this task we must diminish personal political dreaming, acknowledging that the power is 'there' and not 'here'. (Dan,[1] for example, believes that without him, in any case, nothing happens!) It is necessary to listen to that internal spirit, with which we might be able to see, through the USSR, Russia and its life power. We must do this right now. I personally listen – well, I have read in the current newspapers so and so, so and so. I supremely agree … I listen, soon I will write, certainly not about that … It is understood that all this happens because we do not do, or do not do enough of, that which life dictates to us. We must act with thought. We must be helped, and maybe not only in 'Days' but even wider.

Yet, all this is small-scale. It does not satisfy and does not approach the goal. But how to act on a large scale, I am unable to say.

Here is what looms unclearly before me. Forgive me – I will write in favour of intervention, but not military, rather economic.

I can imagine the inevitable future penetration of R. by foreign capital, from which we cannot escape. This intervention as I mentioned above[2] is happening even now, in forms most of all ruinous for Russia. This intervention becomes stronger, so that for the monetary economy in Russia, there will always be real pressure from the West. You see, if there will be quotations on the chervonets[3] in the market, then other solid banks can receive concessions – using them to threaten and to frighten the government. This could be more terrible than Wrangel and the whole military campaign.

Is it thus forbidden for us to use this economic possibility, opening it to the West? Is it forbidden to link economic concessions with our political concessions? I understand and do not deny that it is easier for them to receive profitable concessions from the Soviet regime. But it is virtually certain that, to exploit the concessions (20–30 years!) would be more peaceful and profitable under civil law and order.

It could be interesting to Western recipients of concessions to receive political guarantees, which could include a provision that, one by one, non-Soviet people would be added to the staff of the Soviet regime, to work with the Soviets.

How practical is this to realise?

It is necessary to agree among themselves – that is, all those who can understand how to operate in Russia, who are capable of understanding the New Russia. It requires an honest reaction in West European political activity. It's necessary for them also to forge a certain common front.

These are the thoughts that come to my mind.

Fantastic? Perhaps. But what else is there to do? I am working with all my strength. And if there will not be some perspective, then involuntarily I think of taking myself in hand and transferring my agricultural work to somewhere else, perhaps to Lithuania, perhaps to Estonia.

The other day I saw and talked with arrivals from the south. Everything has become horrible.   There are no higher schools, Russian youth have no higher schooling, all the old professors become more and more demoralized, and the degeneration intensifies. We are afraid. I can't arrange meetings, now, with persons who are in Berlin and with whom I had a close acquaintance. There is no more "thee". They obviously avoid meeting me. I understand them, yet this hurts and vexes. But is anyone to blame for it all?

I do not wish to generalize, but a grain of truth in my experiences undoubtedly exists. We require our daily work, a bite to eat. As for our emigrant life, we hope to break away from it, to observe from the side.

Now, also in letters from you, I find a grain of pessimism.

I write all this personally for you. Would like to know your frame of mind.

If there will be time, write, even though it is brief. I will devour it.

All the best, then. How is the health of Sergei Nikolaevich?

I sent you the other day a postcard with a request for assistance concerning the dispatch of my manuscripts. Do not say no to helping in this matter. Did you not have as a guest Savitskii, whom I asked to arrange a train trip to Berlin of Prague professors, to visit us at the Institute? On the latter – I do not wish to write to the Institute; it is all so tedious and rather disgusting.[4]

We live now to some extent in the country. Ol'ga and Nikita lounge on the banks of the lake – I, at other times, wallow on the sand and go for a swim. I spend much time on the train to Berlin, 5 hours 55 minutes per trip.

Olya sends greetings.

All the best.   A. Ch.

NOTES

1.   Fedor Dan, exiled leader of the Menshevik party, who arrived in Berlin in February, 1922.
2.   Mentioned, perhaps, in the earlier portion of the letter which has been lost.
3.   Lenin's government sought to re-establish a stable currency as part of the New Economic Policy. The new basic unit of currency was backed by gold and named after that used in the time of Peter the Great – the Chernovets.
4.   His Scientific Research Institute had been operating in his absence for a year and a half. This comment indicated that Chayanov already felt the negative elements gathering in his Institute.

ORIGINAL OF LETTER 38 IN CHAYANOV'S OWN HAND

[illegible] 3 II

запад и мысль не покидают.
Если же мы желаем еще раз с Россией
(а я больше всего именно этого хочу), то
и сейчас должны вмешаться.
А вот, как вмешаться и чем вмешаться —
эту задачу разрешить трудно.
В маленьком масштабе еще, пожалуй,
можно разрешить. Пусть они [illegible]
нашу публицистическую работу. Надо [illegible]
[illegible] и объективно разъяснять Россию и СССР.
Надо изучать живые процессы в народном
хозяйстве, даже содействовать этим процес-
сам интеллигенции, работающей с сов.
властью. Если мы этого не сделаем, то
будем выброшены и отрешимся навсегда
с судьбой от России. Какими писаниями
будут путешественниками, пишу и пишут целы
будут там вернее. Нужно обеспечиваться,
при первой [illegible] совокупной возможности роста народного хозяйства выявится
еще ярче, что мы и должны делать, пока
будем иметь возможность.

Но, как Оскар в большом масштабе, я
сказал не читал.

Вот что идёт мне ещё не даёт
покой. Признаюсь, я мечу шагать по индуст-
венному, но не всемирно, а экономи-
чески. Свет представляется мне Адреса
и в будущем приникновение в Р. иностран-
ный капитала. Сами он не выходим.
Эта сопряжения, как я упоминал выше,
шёл и теперь, в наиболее решительном
фоне Госси фермам. Эта сопряжение уси-
ли́т, так как при деловом обороте
в России, давление Рэда Адлер всегда
более решительны. Вот если Адлер не
решёт капиравобрек церковец, то любой
солидный банк может получить кой-
чество — скорее кредиторов и материал.
Эт суда срамные Вранжель и военный
военные площадь!

Так нельзя ли нам также использо-
вать эти экономические возможности...

necessary to break with Russian agrarian circles, or with the agronomic public in which you had confidence before the white heat. Major work is needed to moderate their bellicose zeal.

Apropos, you write of Laur and Brdlik. With the first I am well acquainted personally, and the second I know by talks with Kholman and Auhagen – neither one nor the other, in any case, appears to be a theoretician. This is typical (unreadable) drab style.

The Russian text of the book which you gave to Shlömer is something I need very much, since it is the only full (text) and I would like to take it with me when I leave[3]

10 September 1923.

NOTES

1. The article in question seems to have been 'Die neueste Entwicklung der Agrarökonomie in Russland.' [Tübingen, 1923], probably one of the two articles mentioned in Letter #18. Yashchenko's *NRK* published in mid-1922 a Chayanov article entitled 'In the Sphere of New Currents of Russian Economic Thought'.
2. Chayanov's challenge had no apparent effect on Prokopovich. Basile Kerblay, in his *A.V. Chayanov: Life, Career, Works, 1966*, writes that Prokopovich's 1924 book 'answering' Chayanov, published in Berlin in 1924, 'was ... disappointing, since it did not live up to its claims. It was not, in fact, a new theory of peasant economy but a collection of more or less connected essays on different aspects of this economy before the Revolution.'
3. Chayanov's book on the theory of the peasant economy was written in Russian, and given to Schlömer to be translated for publication in German. Apparently, Schlömer gave it back to Prokopovich when the translation was finished.

Letter 41

? November, 1927   From Paris   To Kuskova and Prokopovich in Prague

Dear Ekaterina Dmitrievna and Sergei Nikolaevich!

I am writing to you from Paris, through which lies our route, on what is, this time, a short journey, and I hasten to send you our warmest heart-felt greetings.

Four years have passed since the last time we met together in Berlin, and in these four years so much water has gone by in the stream of history, that these years seem an eternity.

For Ol'ga and me this has been a time of strained, sometimes inhuman work. Her serious book[1] you no doubt have received, and know. I have written a few (3–4) works, but have achieved very much in the organization of our institute of agricultural economy, (where) we now possess a large house,[2] a library of more than 100,000 books, well-furnished offices. We are settling down to research work and have splendid relations with the scientific centers of the entire world.

All this came about with great difficulty, calling for much strength and time but resulting in small success, thanks to which supplementary work is still required. For a year and a half now I have done nothing in addition to scientific work and even have cut in half my pedagogical duties (turned over the cathedra of agricultural cooperation to A.N. Chelintsev and kept for myself only the organization of the economy). We live in Razumovskii,[3] see almost no-one and practically never go to the theater.

Our family life thrives, and when on Sundays grandfather comes to visit, we give ourselves up to family happiness. Grandfather has grown old, often is in bad health, but every year goes to Kislovodsk[4] and returns from there restored. That's all there is to tell about us.

If I were to write in detail about my scientific work, then I would need to write some dozens of pages, you see, and whether this would interest you I do not know. Indeed it is very narrow, the circle of questions on which I am working – agricultural taxation, prime cost, calculation of land reclamation, the effects of land organization.

All this for me is very important, but scarcely arouses a large or general interest.

We plan to be in Paris no more than a week, and then go on through Italy, perhaps to visit Egypt – the purpose of my travel to Italy and France is to become acquainted with the current state of agricultural economy in terms of scientific and research organization of the productivity of southern cultures and fields. I send you a large greeting! Write about yourselves!

Your A. Chayanov.

Paris (8).

Rue de Penthievre, 13.5

NOTES

1 Teatr Maddokca v Moskve.
2 The Boyar's Mansion.
3 Quarters at the Timiryazevskii (formerly Petrovsko-Razumovskoe) Academy.
4 Kislovodsk, a resort city in the northern Caucasus, famed for its mineral waters.
5 In Paris, they stopped at the Hotel de la Présidence.

Appendix

Chayanov and Socialist Agriculture

Translated by
FRANK BOURGHOLTZER

A.V. Chayanov on 'Calculations and Methods of Determining the Effectiveness of Socialist Agriculture and Farming'.

Letter of 21 June 1931, to the secret police after his arrest and imprisonment.

To: 2 SPO, S.M. Sidorov
From: A. Chayanov.
Plan of Research on the theme: Calculations and methods of Determining the Effectiveness of Socialist Agriculture and Farming.

I. Introduction. Accounting Methods in Socialist Agriculture.
The views of Lenin and other leaders of socialist construction on the significance of accounting in the epoch of socialist reconstruction of the nation's economy.

II. General Part.
A. The purpose of installation and organisation of structures of socialist and capitalist economies, and various transitional forms of the epoch of the socialist reconstruction of agriculture.

(1) The capitalist economy. Structures and forms of circulation of capital peculiar to it, in the Second volume of 'Capital' of K. Marx. Theories of bourgeois economists (Davenport, Niklish and others) and their criticisms.

(2) Economic formations of the transition period.

a) The socialist sector in the first years of the transitional period.

b) Details of the planned economy, with decisive predominance of the socialist sector in the national economy in the epoch after the 15th congress of the party.

(3) Completed forms of socialist organisation of the national economy on the basis of the complete rejection of private economy sectors, and categories of market shackles.

B. Basic economic accounting in each of the mentioned periods.

(1) Formulae for calculation in various modifications of additional values of the capitalist economy. Categories — capitalist amortisation, percents on capital, rents and private profits, a final balance of capitalist enterprises, policies of companies for utilisation of capital.

(2) Formulae for economic calculations in various phases of the socialist economy. The polemic of Varga, Strumilin and others in 1920. The polemic of Mias, Marg, Kissel, Leikhtert and others. Setting the general line of the party.

(3) Basic indicators of the effectiveness of socialist agriculture , and their significance, as in apriori planning, as well as in aposteriori reporting aspects.

a) Industrial plans of individual socialist enterprises, as planned extracts from the general plan of the national economy.

b) Indicators of quantitative and qualitative fulfilment of the plan. Chaining the connection of the degrees of fulfillment and their methods, their illumination for calculation.

c) Indicators of industrial labor.

d) Indicators of norms of the expanded reproduction of national economic capital invested in given economic units.

e) Indicators of prime cost.

f) Indicators of the technical effectiveness of the industrial apparat.

g) Social indicators: wages, cultural and domestic indicators etc., and their particular signficance for taking stock of kolkhozes.

(4) Synthetic judgment of the effectiveness of the work of independent enterprises and fields of the socialist economy. Systematic coefficients.

III Special Part

A Separate elements of calculations and analyses of effectiveness.

(1) Calculations of the extent of fulfilment of the plan. Illumination of the following changes of standards of the plan and the impact of occurrences of 'objective causes' (meteorological conditions, locusts, hail-storms etc.).

(2) Analysis of the balance of enterprises of the socialist sector of the transitional period and the difference from analyses of the balance of capitalist enterprises.

(3) Analysis of the circulation of capital in the socialist economy and norms of broadened reproduction of capital. Problems of the calculation of so-called 'social profitability', its correct and incorrect interpretations.

(4) The notion of productivity of labour in Marxist theory. Formulae of American and European bourgeois economists and their critics. Methods of calculating the productivity of labour projected to the socialist sector of the Soviet national economy.

(5) Calculation and analysis of prime cost in the socialist economy. Prime cost involving products. Method of separating amortization and general expenditures. Measures of precise calculation of prime cost and methods of their approximate calculation. A priori and a posteriori prime cost and the probabilities of coincidence.

(6) Analysis of production and organisational structure of the economy, and methods of construction and analysis of 'Screened Prime Cost'.

(7) Technical indicators: coefficients of the relativity of outputs, coefficients of the utilisation of fuel, coefficients of the utilisation of machines and stationary equipment (their amortisation).

(8) Social indicators: real wages, communal facilities, sanitary conditions, domestic and cultural indicators of the 'Standard of Life' as one of the most important indicators for calculation in the kolkhozes.

B. Expertise of the economy and methods of synthetic judgments as a whole. A succession of processes of expertise, a group of indicators, their calculations and processing. Methods of construction of synthetic indicators, accentuating their formulae for leaders of the organs. Opinions on the quality of the organisationl leadership of the economic path, with constant supervision and daily calculation of the results for many different, but homogeneous sectors of the economy (methods of Grekov and others). Over-estimation and expertise for merging and reorganising enterprises. Expertise on variants of reconstruction.

IV Conclusion.
The evolution of the significance of independent indicators for measurement of the disappearance of private economy sectors and categories of market goals with the transition to legal forms of the socialist economy.

21 VI 31   A. Chayanov
P.S. Several of the questions of these themes of mine began to be elaborated already in articles in 1920. There were, especially, many of these themes of my work in 1929 and 1930 – my work on the calculation of zerno-sovkhozes, for expertise with 8 sovkhozes in the Moscow region, the article 'Methods of appraisal and the success of the work of sovkhozes', in 'Soc.Agriculture', and several chapters in my book, 'Organization of Large-Scale Agriculture.' However, all of these were my first experiments. This work can be finished in 6–8 months.
               A. Ch.
NOTE: The term '2 SPO' is an acronym for the 2nd Secret Political Department, and Sidorov is the agent assigned to deal with Chayanov. It is characteristic of Chayanov to use Latin characters for his outlines, even though the texts are in cyrillic. In Part 3 of II/B, his outline skips from 'f' to 'h', which may be explained by the fact that, in Russian, the 'g' and 'h' are interchangeable, phonetically.

This letter to Sidorov was written two and a half months after Chayanov had been notified that he was guilty of counter-revolutionary crimes. He had been moved from the Lubyanka 'inner prison' to a cell in Butyrki prison, pending his transfer to the political prison in Yaroslavl. He was released from prison in 1932 and sent to Alma Ata, in Kazakhstan, where he was allowed to work in the university and, eventually, with the Kazakh Commissariat of Agriculture until his re-arrest and execution in 1937, but there is no record of any further work on this plan for the evaluation of socialist agriculture.

5

Biographical Glossary

FRANK BOURGHOLTZER

Note: This Biographical Glossary consists of entries for those individuals who appear in the foregoing text, and about whom the reader who is not a specialist in Russian studies may know little. The entries are, for the most part, brief. Some, however, are necessarily rather longer than others. One in particular, that for Sergei Nikolaevich Prokopovich, is particularly detailed. The relationship between Chayanov and Prokopovich was especially important and this called for more detailed treatment of Prokopovich.

Agranov (Sorendzon),Yakov Saulovich (1893–1937), played a leading role in many prosecutions: from that which resulted in the execution of the poet, Nikolai Gumilev, in 1922, to the 'show trials' of the later 1920s and 1930s. Nadezhda Mandelshtam believed him to be the chief of a 'literary department' of the OGPU. In the case of the so-called 'Toiling Peasant Party', Agranov began his interrogation of Chayanov on 5 August 1930. In mid-September, after 13 sessions, Agranov turned the interrogation over to an assistant, Aleksandr Slavatinskii. On 6 April 1931, Chayanov was pronounced guilty of leading the 'Toiling Peasant Party' in counter-revolutionary activity aimed at overthrowing the Soviet regime with the help of foreign intervention. Agranov rose to almost the highest level of the Secret Police apparatus, high enough to be assigned to an apartment within the Kremlin itself. He was intimately involved in the events surrounding the murder of the Leningrad party chief, Sergei Kirov, an affair that led to the period of Stalin's rule known as the 'Great Terror'. Agranov himself became a victim of the Terror. In his trial, he was accused – ironically – of falsifying evidence in such prosecutions as that of the 'Toiling Peasant Party', when Chayanov was convicted. One of the chief witnesses to testify against Agranov was Aleksandr Slavatinskii, the agent who had followed Agranov as Chayanov's inquisitor.

Arnol'd, Vladimir Fedorovich (1872–?), economist and statistician, 'liberal narodnik'; one of the earliest economists to develop mathematical procedures, the use of correlations, to analyse the income of family farms from agriculture.

Auhagen, Otto Georg (1869–1945), professor in Berlin at the Institute of Agriculture, well-versed in Russian agricultural history and practice. From 1900 to 1906, he served as agricultural officer in the German embassy in Petersburg, and, again, from 1927 to 1930, in the German embassy in Moscow. A top-secret note from the OGPU, dated May of 1931, was entitled 'The Anti-Soviet Activities of Prof. Augagen'. It stated that the Ministry of Foreign Affairs wanted no action of an official nature to be taken against Auhagen, since such measures 'would bring about serious protests from the German press and from the German Social Democrats'. Auhagen was one of Chayanov's closest associates in Germany; and wrote a preface for the 1923 German edition of his *The Theory of Peasant Economy.*

Bakhmetev, Boris Aleksandrovich (1880–1952) had been appointed by the Provisional Russian government to be ambassador to the United States. After the Bolshevik coup, he became an important link between the Russian emigrant community and sources of assistance in the United States.

Baxrax, Aleksandr Vasilievich (1902–87), Russian journalist working for several Russian language newspapers in Berlin in the period of its literary and artistic efflorescence at the time of Lenin's expulsion of Russian intellectuals. As the secretary of the 'House of Arts', he came to know Kuskova when she arrived in Berlin, and Osorgin when he arrived three months later. When Kuskova and Osorgin decided to join the movement to create an alternative to the 'House of Arts', more in the tradition of Moscow's 'Writer's Club', Baxrax joined them, becoming secretary of the new organisation. Through Kuskova, he came to know Chayanov and his fantastic novellas. When the Russian intellectuals began to leave, at the end of 1923, Baxrax stayed on in Berlin for a number of years, then moved to Paris, where he published, in 1979, his book of memoirs, *Po Pamiati, Po*

Zapisim. Literaturnie Portrety (*From Memory, From Notes. Literary Portraits*).

Bellamy, Edward (1850–98), American author of socialist literature, including *Looking Backward*.

Bellmer Hans (1902–75), German painter and lithographer, specialised in erotic paintings and constructions, produced 'artificial girls'. He fled to Paris in 1938, and joined the French surrealists.

Belyi, Andrei (Boris N. Bugayev, 1880–1934), Russian poet and novelist, son of a mathematician, considered by some to be the chief theoretician of the symbolists. He became a follower of Rudolf Steiner and his 'anthroposophy', went to Switzerland in 1914 to live briefly in an anthroposophical community. Back in Russia, he viewed the Bolshevik revolution as a preparation for a Second Coming, became disillusioned and went to Berlin in 1921, where his wife left him to join Steiner. The Russian novelist Zamyatin wrote: 'Mathematics, poetry, anthroposophy, fox-trot – these are some of the sharpest angles that make up the fantastic image of Andrei Belyi.'

Blatchford, Robert (1851–1943), English socialist.

Bukharin, Nikolai Ivanovich (1899–1938) was the most talented technocrat in Lenin's inner circle. In April, 1922, during a Comintern congress in Berlin, Bukharin, and his colleague, Karl Radek, promised the other delegates that death penalties would not be sought in the trial of the Socialist Revolutionaries. Lenin condemned the agreement. At the trial, Bukharin suggested clemency – on the ground of 'political expediency'. The death penalty was imposed on 15 of the defendants, one of whom, S.D. Morozov, committed suicide in the Lubyanka prison a year and a half later. In early 1924, the sentences of the other 14 were reduced to five years imprisonment. In 1937, any of the former defendants who were still alive were shot. In 1938, as a result of the most celebrated of the show-trials, Bukharin was shot..

Buryshkin, P.A., author on the subject of the history of Russian philosophy and religious thought. Published in 1954 *Moskva Kupecheskaya.*

Braikevich, Mikhail Vladimirovich (?–1940), engineer, economist, follower of Milyukov's Cadet party, served in the Provisional government after the February revolution. In the 1920s, Milyukov persuaded him to emigrate. In London, he directed a Russian economic society, whose members included Left Cadets, Narodny Socialists, former Socialist Revolutionaries.

Brutskus, Ber Davidovich (1878–1938), economist and agronomist, professor at the Institute of Agriculture in Petrograd. He approved of the Stolypin reforms, was interested in the study of the labour farm but a critic of 'Narodniks'. Emigrated in 1922.

Bulgakov, Mikhail Afanasevich (1891–1940), novelist and playwright. His novel, *Heart of a Dog,* featured a physician who specialised in the transplanting of body parts, and who tried planting a human brain into a dog. Ellendea Proffer, describing the Moscow that Bulgakov found on his arrival in the first years of the 1920s, wrote: 'It is hard for a Western reader to comprehend the degree to which the housing shortage shaped life in Moscow in those years. The city was overwhelmed by people pouring in from the provinces, sure that things must be better in the capital. This was the year of the terrible Volga famine, and many regions were still devastated by the war.' Several of Bulgakov's stories of this period were published under the title: *A Treatise on Housing.* The *Treatise* stories, along with many other Bulgakov stories, were first published by the Berlin journal, *Nakanune,* whose Moscow office was frequented by Bulgakov and other writers who survived largely on their sales to the 'Changing Landmarks' journal. His best-known novel, *The Master and Margarita,* was influenced by one of Chayanov's fanciful novelettes.

Chagall, Marc (1887–1985), Russian artist, born in Vitebsk of a devoutly Jewish family, an influence that became an important part of his distinctive style. He studied in Petersburg, went to Paris in 1910. He returned to Russia for a visit just before war was declared in 1914 and was unable to leave until 1922. He lived in Berlin in 1922–23, in Paris until 1940, and in the United States until 1947 when he returned to France.

Chelintsev, Aleksandr Nikolaevich (1874–1962), one of the founders of the Organization-Production school; a close colleague of Chayanov's, participated in budget analyses of agriculture, worked on agrarian reforms in the Provisional Government of 1917. Worked on farm organisation and on problems of co-operation, differentiation of the peasantry and family-farm theory.

Chernenkov, Nikolai Nikolaevich (1863–?), statistician; worked with the Cadet party, one of the forerunners of the Organization-Production school.

Chernov, Viktor Mikhailovich (1873–1952), founder of the Socialist Revolutionary party in 1902, sometimes called 'The Robespierre of the Russian Revolution'. The Socialist Revolutionaries essentially carried on, in the Twentieth Century, the Nineteenth Century traditions of the Narodniks. Minister of Agriculture in the Provisional government after the February revolution. Elected president of the Constituent Assembly at the end of 1917. Took part in attempt to establish a non-Bolshevik Russian government, barely escaped with his life. In Berlin, became editor of the short-lived S-R newspaper *Golos Rossii*. He and Aleksandr Kerenskii accused each other of failures that led to the Bolshevik coup.

Danilov, Viktor Petrovitch (1925–), historian, Professor at the Institute of Russian History in Moscow; head of the Center for Peasant and Rural Studies at the Interdisciplinary Academic Centre for Social Sciences; leader for the research project 'The Peasant Revolution in Russia, 1902–1922'. He has concentrated much of his attention on the course of agriculture in Russia, and on Aleksandr Chayanov in particular. He wrote the preface for a re-publication in 1991 of Chayanov's *Theory of Peasant Cooperatives*.

Dubrovskii, Sergei Mitrofanovich (1900–70), historian-economist, Marxist. Entered the Institute of Red Professors in 1921. Served briefly as the Dean of the Faculty of Economics of the Timiriazev Academy, then became Assistant Director of the International Agrarian Institute, and Deputy Director of the Peasant International. In 1934, he began to teach as Dean of the Faculty of History at Leningrad University. He was sent into exile in 1937, returned in 1954, served at the Institute of History and the Academy of Sciences in Moscow. He was a leading critic of the Organization-Production school in general , and of Aleksandr Chayanov in particular.

Duncan, Isadora (1878–1927), see **Yesenin, Evgenii**

Ehrenburg, Ilya (1891–1967), Russian novelist and journalist. In 1908, as a teenager, he fled to Paris from Russia to escape prosecution for revolutionary activities. He lived in Paris until the 1917 revolutions allowed him to return to Russia, where he became a noted apologist for the policies of both Lenin and Stalin. He spent much of his life abroad, and was living and writing in Berlin from 1921 to 1924, the period that included Chayanov's stay in Germany. He refused to write for the 'Changing Landmarks' journal, *Nakanune*. In 1955, his novel, *The Thaw*, attracted attention both in Russia and in the West, not so much for its literary quality as for the label it gave to the process of de-Stalinisation.

Figner, Vera (1852–1942), daughter of a noble family and a revolutionary of the 1800s, she was arrested in 1883 on a charge of complicity in the assassination of the Tsar Aleksandr II. She served 20 years in the dungeons of the Schlusselburg fortress in St. Petersburg, and wrote a widely-read, widely-praised book based on her life in prison: *Memories of a Revolutionist*. In Paris, in 1910, she joined a Society to Help Political Prisoners in Russia. After the February revolution in 1917, she was active politically, became an honorary member of the Moscow committee of the 'Political Red Cross', and a member of a literary cooperative, 'Zapruga', whose membership included Alexei Tolstoi, Mikhail Osorgin, Sergei Prokopovich and Ekaterina Kuskova.

Fourier, Charles (1772–1837). French socialist-utopian.

France, Anatole (Anatole-Francois Thibault) (1844–1924), one of the most respected authors of France, received the Nobel prize in 1921. Under the influence of a mistress of socialist leanings, and of the socialist politician, Jean Jaures, Anatole France became a pacifist, a supporter of the Russian Revolution and of the French Communist Party. He and Gorkii were good friends.

Fridrikhson, Lev Khristoforovich, colleague at NKZ, assigned to permanent duty in Berlin.

Gessen, Sergei Iosifovich (1887–1950), philosopher, pedagogue, political theorist.

Gippius, Zinaida (1869–1945), symbolist poet, the wife of Dmitri Merezhkovsky (1865–1941), a pioneer of symbolism.

Gorkii, Maksim (Alexei Maksimovich Peshkov 1868–1936), Russian writer of books and plays, best known in literary terms as a master of fiction depicting real life, as in *The Lower Depths*, and *Twenty-Six Men and a Girl*. In personal terms, he was beloved by fellow writers, seeming never to refuse help and/or advice when asked. Politically, he was a sometimes lukewarm, sometimes passionate supporter of the Communist regime. In 1921, after Lenin had ordered the arrest of most of the members of the Committee to Aid the Hungry, many of whom were Gorkii's personal friends, Gorkii was forced to leave Moscow on 'vacation'. He settled in Berlin, from where he voiced in no uncertain terms his condemnation of Lenin's banishment of hundreds of Russia's intellectual elite. Among those who suffered were his warm friends, Kuskova and Prokopovich. At the end of the 1920s, Gorkii returned to Russia, to be greeted as a hero. In his final years, he supported Stalin and Stalin's policies. Kuskova, in the 1930s, wrote a biography, entitled *The Tragedy of Maksim Gorkii.*

Grigoreva, Elena Vasilevna, Chayanov's 'first love', and first wife, whom he had married just before his departure on a European trip in 1912.

Gropius, Walter Adolf (1883–1969), German architect who, in 1918, founded a school to study architecture, and art, in terms of modern technology and new materials. The school was installed in the city of Weimar, and was called the 'Bauhaus'. Gropius, and many others associated with his school, powerfully influenced both modern art and modern architecture.

Grosz, George (1893–1959), German painter, engraver, produced violently anti-war drawings after World War I, attacking social corruption in Germany, and especially the middle class, the Prussian military class, prostitutes and capitalists. He worked with John Heartfeld and Raoul Haussmann in the invention of Photomontage. In 1933, he settled in the United States, returning to Germany only in 1958, shortly before his death.

Herzen, Aleksandr Ivanovich (Yakovlev, 1812–70), revolutionary writer of the early and mid-nineteenth Century. Twice exiled, internally, by the Tsarist government. In 1847, he left Russia, and lived in France, Switzerland and England. His 'Free Russian Press' in London published books, pamphlets and periodicals that he was able to have distributed in Russia, and which contributed to the development of revolutionary tendencies in Russia. His principal publication, *The Bell*, sometimes even appeared on the Tsar's breakfast table. It was in *The Bell* that Herzen responded to the action of the Cossacks in driving rebellious students out of the University of St. Petersburg. To these 'exiles from knowledge', as he called the dispossessed students, Herzen counselled: 'Go to the People'.

Hoffmann, E.T.A. (Ernst Theodor Amadeus, originally Wilhelm, 1776–1822), German author, composer, illustrator, best known for his fanciful, grotesque, imaginative short stories. A number of Russia's most talented young writers began to call themselves 'The Serapion Brothers' in honour of one of Hoffmann's collections with that title. There is no record that Chayanov had any special relationship with these Russian 'Serapion' writers, but he did preface his first fanciful tale, *The Story of the Hairdresser's Mannequin,* with the notice: 'In honour of the great master Ernst Teodor Amadeya Hoffmann the author dedicates his modest work.'

Jevons, William Stanley (1835–82), celebrated English, early neo-classical economist; author of *The Theory of Political Economy.* Suggested a 'balance between "need" and "labour"', upon which Chayanov claimed to draw.

Kandinskii, Vasilii (1866–1944), a native of Moscow, he studied painting in Munich and became a pioneer of abstract art. Like Marc Chagall, he spent the years 1914–21 in Russia, then returned to Berlin, became a professor at the Bauhaus in Weimar. In 1933, after the Nazi regime closed the Bauhaus, Kandinskii settled in Paris.

Kerblay, Basile H. as chair of Russian and Soviet Civilization at the Sorbonne, in Paris, played a major role in the 1960s, seeking out and restoring to public view the forgotten works of Chayanov. The procedure had begun with his colleague at the Sorbonne, Professor Daniel Thorner. An Indian scholar, Dr Zakir Husain, had called Thorner's attention to an important work on the theory of the peasant farm, authored by a mysterious 'Shayanoff'. Professor Thorner traced the name to Chayanov and, with Kerblay and Professor R.E.F. Smith of the University of Birmingham, found a copy of Chayanov's *Theory of the Peasant Farm.* They arranged for publication of an English version in 1966. Kerblay, meanwhile, followed the trail to Moscow where he was able to ferret out , and reprint, 8 volumes of Chayanov's works.

Kerenskii, Aleksandr Fedorovich (1881–1970), a spell-binding public speaker and a member of a splinter group in the Socialist Revolutionary Party, called the 'Labour Wing'. He became a member of the Provisional Government after the February Revolution, when other revolutionary parties refused to take part. He was thus the only important member of the Provisional Government who also was a member of the opposition body, the

Petrograd Soviet. Kerenskii became Prime Minister in mid-1917, attempted to oust the Bolsheviks after their coup, but failed, and fled to the West. (See Chernov). In Berlin, he edited one of the more successful emigré newspapers, *Dni (Days)*. Eventually settled in the United States, died in New York City in 1970.

Khodasevich, Vladislav Felitsianovich (1886–1939), Russian symbolist poet, fascinated by death. He considered the revolution to be but an example of the world's inability to resolve itself into spirits of pure beauty. With Gorkii's help, he left Russia for Berlin in 1922, where he associated with Gippius and the stridently anti-Bolshevik circles. After a relatively short stay in Berlin, he left to settle in Paris.

Khryashcheva, Anna Ivanovna (1868–1934), statistician, developed a methodology of census-taking.

Klepikov, Sokrat Aleksandrovich (1895–1978), bibliophile, known internationally as a connoisseur of filigree, stamps and watermarks. He worked in various literary and art institutions, including the All-Russian House of Books, the Lenin Library, the Government Literary Museum. Klepikov was a first cousin of Aleksandr Chayanov. He and his family were among the closest friends of Chayanov and his family. Klepikov also devoted much time to activity in agricultural studies. As an economist, he took part in the 1917 League of Agrarian Reform, drew up atlases and maps of agricultural activity, published various works, including one with Chayanov (*Nutrition of Russian Peasantry,* including articles of A.V. Chayanov, 1920).

Knipovich, Boris Nikolaevich (1890–1924), economist, statistician, worked in the Ministry of Agriculture of the Provisional government after the February Revolution. After November, 1918, he worked for Narkomzem on matters of agricultural economy, and statistics. He taught in Chayanov's Research Institute, and worked on studies of peasant differentiation.

Koffod, Andrei Andreevich (1850–1945), Danish economist, was attached to the Russian department of agriculture during the Stolypin period, published several works on the subject of village agriculture. Koffod was friendly with Chayanov during Chayanov's stay in Germany, and the acquaintance continued when Koffod became agricultural secretary at the

Danish embassy in Moscow. This relationship was used to support charges of treason against Chayanov. (See **Ushakova**.)

Kondrat'ev, Nikolai Dmitrievich (1892–1938), prominent economist, statistician, universally known for his development of a theory of economic cycles, known as 'Kondrat'ev Waves'. His early education, in St. Petersburg, was in Church schools, but, in 1906, he was dismissed from the Seminary for political 'unreliability', and joined the Socialist Revolutionary Party. He was arrested in 1906 and spent seven months in jail. At the University in Petrograd, one of his teachers was M.I. Tugan-Baranovskii. He graduated in 1915, taught in the university's division of political economy and statistics, working part-time at the office of the Petrograd Zemstvo Union. In the first days of the February revolution, he joined the Commission of Food Supplies, and continued to work there much of 1917, as well as being active in the League of Agrarian Reform and other peasant-related organizations. In this capacity, he became acquainted with S.N. Prokopovich, who served in the Provisional Government as Minister of Food Supply. After the Bolshevik Revolution, it was Kondrat'ev who signed the final order of the Food Ministry. After the Bolshevik closure of the Constituent Assembly, Kondrat'ev left Petrograd. In Moscow, he joined Prokopovich's Cooperative Institute at the Shaniavskii University, took part in the Congress of the All-Russian Council of Cooperatives, began to teach at the Petrovskii Agricultural Academy. In all of these activities, he worked with Chayanov and his colleagues. When Chayanov created his Research Institute, Kondrat'ev was invited to set up within it a 'Laboratory of Marketing'. one of the first in the world. Chayanov not only invited Kondrat'ev to join him in his Institute, he also arranged for Kondrat'ev to join the Commissariat of Agriculture. In 1924, Kondrat'ev and his wife were sent on a foreign tour, similar to Chayanov's trip to Europe in 1922-23. The Kondrat'evs visited Germany, England, Canada and the United States. Kondrat'ev and Chayanov were the two most influential academic forces in Russian agriculture in the period that preceded the swing to Stalinism. They acknowledged and admired one another's abilities, but there also was an element of jealousy. Temperamentally, they were opposites: Chayanov an extrovert who enjoyed performing, enjoyed the company of people; Kondrat'ev, an introvert, absorbed in private thoughts. Kondrat'ev's daughter has described how she used to look forward, as a little girl, to invitations to join Chayanov on one of his walking tours of historical Moscow, during which he would enthral his group with descriptions of things that had happened, historical figures who had done things at the various houses, parks, street corners of his favourite city. Her father never did anything like that. When Kondrat'ev and Chayanov were accused of being the leaders of the 'Toiling Peasant Party', it was Kondrat'ev who was made to appear as the principal culprit, and his prison sentence was more severe than Chayanov's. Ultimately, both were executed, but whereas Chayanov had a few years of relative freedom in internal exile, Kondrat'ev never had a single day of freedom until he was shot on 17 September 1938.

Krasin, Leonid Borisovich (1870–1926) was one of Lenin's close comrades in the earliest days of Bolshevism, using the conspiratorial name of Nikitch. Krasin left the party after the 1905 revolution to become a businessman, in the employ of Siemens-Schukert Electrical Company, first in Berlin, then in St. Petersburg. As a favour to Lenin, after the Bolshevik coup of 1917, he helped in the negotiation of the peace treaty with Germany, became the dominant figure in the postwar effort to restore trade, teamed with the British Prime Minister Lloyd George to arrange a World Economic Conference in Genoa, Italy. While there is little or no documentation to illustrate a personal relationship between Krasin and Chayanov, there were at least three areas in the lives of each that seemed to dovetail: (i) Both men reacted energetically to the post-revolution wave of pillage and destruction of everything connected with Russia's past. In Petrograd, soon after the February revolution of 1917, Krasin created a body known as the 'Expert Commission', which inspected, valued, catalogued and preserved objects of high artistic and historical merit [*O'Connor*: 127]. At the First All-Russian Cooperative Congress in Moscow, in February of 1918, Chayanov called on all Russian co-operators to work for the preservation of Russia's artistic culture. A committee was formed for this purpose, with Chayanov as one of its most active leaders. (ii) At the same All-Russian Cooperative Congress, Chayanov startled the delegates with a speech entitled 'The Basic Task of Cooperatives in the Organization of Exports.' His colleagues ridiculed him, but Krasin would subsequently apply that very concept to undermine the Western economic blockade of Russia, using agricultural exports as a source of hard currency and using co-operative organisations to conduct trade relations in the absence of formal diplomatic relations with the West. Chayanov was a key figure in the Central Association of Consumer Societies (*Tsentrosoyuz*), a major element in Krasin's conduct of trade; (iii) Krasin was by far the chief proponent and activist in the policy of encouraging Russia's technical intelligentsia to work with the Bolshevik regime in the interest of Russia's future prosperity. Chayanov and his colleagues were especially relevant examples of this technical intelligentsia, and Chayanov, who considered himself a 'non-party socialist', felt it his duty to apply his expertise to the development of the economy, no matter who was politically in charge. In 1928, when he wrote a screenplay and helped to produce a film – *Albidum* – *Victory over the Sun* – about agriculture, his 'hero' was an agricultural scientist, developing a revolutionary theory for the production of grain, working against time to produce a large crop for export. In the film's climax, the grain was triumphantly loaded aboard a ship bound for foreign markets, and the name of the ship was the 'Leonid B. Krasin'. See **Rashit Marvanovich Yangirov**.

Krestinskii, Nikolai Nikolaievich (1883–1938), former member of Lenin's politburo and Commissar of Finance. After the Rapallo agreement, he became the first USSR ambassador to Germany.

Kritsman, Lev Natanovich (1890–1938), a historian, became the leader of the Agrarian Marxists in their campaign to discredit Chayanov and claim for themselves the leadership in agricultural theory and policy. He challenged the validity of Khryashcheva's work, claiming that her theories had been rendered invalid by changing conditions following the Bolshevik revolution [*Cox*: 12]. Kritsman presided over the public vilification of Chayanov at an Agrarian Marxist conference at the end of 1939. A few years later, Kritsman and his Agrarian Marxists also fell from favour.

Kuraev, B. B. (1892–1938), became head of the Narkomzem committee for co-operatives in 1919. Served as editor of the Narkomzem journal until 1921, then joined the staff of the newspaper *Pravda*. When the members of the Famine Committee were arrested, Kuraev wrote in *Pravda*, to Kuskova's dismay, that 'many members of the Committee were ashamed of their membership, and concealed it.'

Kushchenko, Georgii Aleksandrovich (1878–?), statistician, developed methods of dynamic analysis of peasant farms, using statistics collected from 1882 to 1911 in the Surazh uezd of the Chernigovskii guberniia.

Kuskova, Ekaterina Dmitrievna (1869–1958) crossed swords with her fellow Marxist revolutionary, Vladimir Ulianov, even before he had begun to call himself Lenin. She wrote a political document that infuriated him. She was just a year older than he. Both were products of the movement, inspired by Aleksandr Herzen's admonition to 'go to the people (the Narod)', in reponse to Tsarist oppression. Some 'Narodniks' sought to help peasants, to improve their standard of living. Other Narodniks sought to use the peasants' discontent to fuel a socialist revolution. Georgii Plekhanov parted company with the Narodnik revolutionaries when he decided that a Marxist solution, based upon a powerful proletariat, was ideologically superior, and because he felt that the terrorist program the Narodniks had adopted was 'a waste of time'. Ulyanov became a disciple of Plekhanov. Kuskova, having begun her revolutionary experience as a Narodnik, was arrested in 1893 for distributing 'criminal literature', and spent a month in prison in Nizhnii Novgorod. Following this experience, Kuskova also left the Narodniks to join Plekhanov's movement. In 1898, that movement received a name – 'The Social Democratic (Revolutionary) Worker's Party'. Its members were united in their general acceptance of Marxism, but divided in their interpretations. Petr Struve, who actually wrote the manifesto of the new party, believed firmly that the development of bourgeois capitalism was a necessary first stage on the path to socialism. Ulianov agreed with that, but did not agree with Struve's apparent willingness to make capitalism an end in itself. E.H. Carr points to Struve's admonition that socialists should avoid unealistic projects of 'heaven-storming', and should 'learn in the school of capitalism'. As a result of their differences with Ulianov, Struve and his followers became known as 'Legal Marxists'. Later, Struve joined the party of' Konstitutional Democrats – Cadets'. Another segment of the new party questioned the ability of the Russian proletariat to comprehend intellectually what was involved in a socialist revolution. Kuskova wrote down her thoughts on this subject, intending mainly to clarify her own thinking. She suggested that two matters were involved – economics and politics. The proletariat would be interested only in economic concerns – better working conditions, social improvements. It would have no experience on which to base an understanding of the politics involved. All that Russian Marxists could do, she wrote, was to support the economic struggle of the proletariat and participate on the workers' behalf in liberal opposition activity. The effect was that intellectuals in the party were limited to the same goals as bourgeois liberals. Friends of Ulianov, who was at this time in exile in Siberia, rushed a copy of Kuskova's essay to him, and he rushed a denunciation of it back to St Petersburg. He called Kuskova's work a 'Credo' for 'Economists'. Party members who agreed with her 'Credo', all came to be called 'Economists'. His response became the basis of an essay published later, when he had adopted his pseudonym, 'Lenin'', under the title 'What Is To Be Done?'

Laur, Professor Ernst Ferdinand (1871–1964), Swiss economist, chairman of the Swiss Peasant Union and leader of the Swiss Peasant Secretariat in 1898; helped to organise the so-called Black Peasant International in 1923. He originated theories on the organisation of agricultural enterprises, on agricultural taxation and on agrarian policies. Chayanov dated the origin of his book on the *Peasant Economy* as the year 1912, when, as a young economist, he spent time with Professor Laur in Zurich, working with Laur's system of collecting budget information, a system Chayanov later criticized.

Litoshenko, Lev Nikolaevich (1886–1936), economist, worked on budget analyses of peasant farms. He and Chayanov were fellow professors at the Timiryazevskii Agricultural Academy, and Litoshenko also became a leading member of Chayanov's Research Institute. Litoshenko strongly opposed Chayanov's concept of a labour–consumption balance. He coined the term 'neonarodnik' as a sarcastic characterisation of Chayanov, comparing the Organization-Production school's emphasis on the family farm with the interests of the early *narodniks* of the nineteenth century. In October of 1923, as Chayanov was leaving Berlin, Litoshenko passed through the city on his way to an International Statistical Congress in Brussels, followed by a ten-day stay in Paris. Litoshenko was arrested and imprisoned at the same time as Chayanov, on essentially the same charges, and, like Chayanov, was shot in 1937.

Lloyd George, David (1863–1945), Liberal politician, responsible for the introduction of national health and unemployment insurance before World War I, and Home Rule for Ireland after the war. During the war, he was, first, Secretary of State for War, and then Prime Minister. He was one of the framers of the Versailles treaty, and supported the idea of trade with Russia under certain conditions. He worked with Krasin to bring about the Genoa conference, and approved of a *de facto* recognition of the new Soviet state. His government was overturned in the autumn of 1922 as a result of Conservative protests against Irish home rule and against his relatively liberal policies toward Russia.

Maddox, Mikhail Egorovich is described in Ol'ga Chayanov's pamphlet as an Englishman, formerly a professor at Oxford University. He appeared in the court of Catherine the Great in 1766 as an instructor in mathematics and French to Catherine's son, Paul. In the 1770s, he was prominent in Moscow's world of entertainment, specialising in mechanical innovations for the stage. His ambition was to build his own theatre. In due course, he did just that. His theatre was called the 'Maddox Petrovskii Theatre'. It would subsequently be called the 'Bolshoi (Great) Petrovskii Theatre', and, finally, on 6 (19) January of 1825, the 'Moscow Bolshoi Theatre'. Ol'ga Chayanov's pamphlet was prepared for the 100th anniversary of that opening night, in January of 1925.

Mayakovskii, Vladimir Vladimirovich (1893–1930), Russian artist, poet, futurist, acclaimed by Stalin as the greatest poet of the revolution, although his greatest work was not about politics, but about life, and love. In 1922, he took part in a major exhibition in Berlin of Russian art, displaying ten of his own whimsical propaganda posters, featuring his own drawings and his own couplets, popularising government policies. More than 500 works of art were displayed at the Van Diemen gallery, and musical events were staged, featuring among others, Prokofiev. Mayakovskii, through his friendship with Prokofiev and the ballet-master Diaghilev, who was also part of the pro-Russian exhibit in Berlin, received a visa to go on to Paris for a visit. Chayanov's son, Vasilii, recalls his mother describing a meeting she and Chayanov had in Riga, on their way to their European sojourn. In fact, they left Moscow early in April of 1922, and, although Mayakovskii's first trip outside of Russia was to Riga , it took place only in May. Mayakovskii made a second trip abroad, to Berlin, in October of 1922. He travelled through Petrograd to Revel (Tallin), from where he sailed by ship to Stettin, and thence to Berlin. At this same time, Chayanov and his wife were leaving England and travelling to Berlin. It is conceivable that they might have met Mayakovskii, but it could only have been after their arrival in Berlin.

Makarov, Nikolai Pavlovich (1887–1980), graduated from the economic department of the Law Faculty of Moscow University in 1911; began work with budgetary studies of Russian farms, joined Chayanov and Prokopovich at the Shanyavskii University, and at the Linen Cooperative Centre. He participated in the study of co-operative organisation, became a leading member of the Organization-Production school. From 1920 to 1924, he studied agricultural production in the United States and Western Europe. He became a professor at the Timiryazevskii Academy in 1924. In 1930, he was arrested as an alleged member of the 'Toiling Peasant Party', and shared a cell with Chayanov in the Yaroslavskii prison. He was not, however, sentenced to death.

Malevich, Kasimir (1878–1935), a devotee of abstract art, he began painting peasant subjects in 1909; became completely abstract in 1915 with a style that he called 'Suprematism', worked with Chagall in Vitebsk in 1919.

Medvedev, Zhores, biologist, geneticist whose stubborn resistance to the flawed theories of T.D. Lysenko forced him to leave Russia and take up his work in England. Author of *Soviet Agriculture* (1987) , as well as several books with his brother, the Russian historian, Roy Medvedev.

Milyukov, Pavel Nikolaevich (1859–1943), principal theoretician of the party of Konstitutional Democrats, became foreign minister of the Provisional government set up after the abdication in 1917 of the Tsar, but resigned when his policy of continuing the war against Germany lost favour. After the Bolshevik coup, he attended a conference in Jasny, Rumania, to discuss resistance to the Bolshevik regime, and went, as a member of a small delegation, to Paris, to request Western intervention. The delegates were rejected by the French. Milyukov remained abroad, and began to publish his own newspaper in Paris, *Poslednie Novosti*, in April of 1920. In 1921, he announced that it was time for a 'new tactic', time to renounce the idea of armed struggle against the Bolsheviks. This stand drove the rightists in his Cadet party toward the Monarchists. The left wing gravitated toward the Socialist Revolutionaries.

More, Thomas (1478–1535), English Utopian-socialist, introduced the term 'Utopia'.

Muenzenberg, Willi, an organiser for revolutionary socialists in Stuttgart, caught Lenin's attention and was appointed, first, as head of the Communist Youth International, and then as founder of another organisation, called International Workers' Aid. Eventually, Muenzenberg built his positions into a 'Soviet–German communications empire' [*Willett*, 1978].

Nabokov, Vladimir Vladimirovich (1899–1977), Russian novelist who lived and wrote as an émigré in Germany for ten years, but never wrote in German. He did later write, very successfully, in English. In Berlin, he wrote under a pseudonym (V. Sirin). His father, Vladimir Nabokov, was a co-editor of the Russian language newspaper in Berlin, *Rul'*. On 28 March 1922, Nabokov's father was one of the hosts at a gala reception for Pavel Milyukov, who was visiting Berlin, when a would-be assassin tried to kill

Milyukov. The elder Nabokov threw himself between Milyukov and the assailant. He was mortally wounded.

Nansen, Fridtjof (1861–1930), Norwegian arctic explorer, much admired by Russians., including Lenin. Worked to help refugees during the First World War, became High Commissioner for Refugee Affairs for the League of Nations. The Nansen Committee worked with the American Relief Administration. in Russian famine relief. The Committee also began to issue 'Nansen Passports' to émigrés, which were, in effect, passports for stateless people, recognised by all members of the League of Nations.

Nezhdanova, Antonina Vasilievna (1873–?), one of Russia's greatest coloratura sopranos, who entered the Bolshoi Theatre company in 1902 to begin a 40-year career. She sang with all the great artists of her time – Chaliapin and Caruso among others – in Russia and abroad, including the Grand Opera in Paris.s. After the Bolshevik Revolution, Nezhdanova joined Konstantin Sergeievich Stanislavskii in an experiment to apply his principles of acting to the opera. In the mid-1920s, she and her husband, Bolshoi orchestra conductor V. Golovanov, joined the co-operative dacha community overlooking the Moscow River, organised by Chayanov and two of his friends.

Nikolaevskii, Boris I. (1888–1937). Chayanov's reference to Nikolaevskii in Letters – 5 – indicates that he was familiar with Yashchenko's friend and collaborator, Boris Nikolaevskii, and was aware that Nikolaevskii already was collecting archival materials. Nikolaevskii, a dissident Bolshevik, arrived in Berlin in 1922 and became a member of the editorial board, as well as archivist, for Aleksandr Yashchenko's journal, *Novaya Russkaya Kniga*. Nikolaevskii's archival activities were carried on for many years, in Berlin, and then in Paris after the demise of Russian Berlin. His archive, eventually, became a major part of the collections in the Hoover Institution at Stanford University. In the 1930s, Nikolaevskii had a long series of heart-to-heart conversations in Paris with Nikolai Bukharin on the subject of Bukharin's concerns about Stalin's leadership. Nikolaevskii published, anonymously, an extremely controversial 'Letter from an Old Bolshevik', detailing the dissatisfactions of party members in Moscow with Stalin.

Nikonov, Aleksandr Aleksandrovich (1918–95), agrarian economist, president of VASKHNIL (All-Russian Academy of Agricultural Science named for Lenin), and director of the Agrarian Institute; took the initiative in 1985, with the personal help of Mikhail Gorbachev, to push to a conclusion the rehabilitation by the Supreme Military Court of Chayanov and his fellow victims of the Toiling Peasant Party prosecution.

Novgorodtsev, Pavel Ivanovich (1866–1924), a jurist and social philosopher, expelled under the same Leninist decree as Propokovich and others. He was a critic of scientific socialism, and a proponent of existentialism and a Christian approach to matters of ethics.

Oganovskii, Nikolai Petrovich (1874–1938), agrarian economist, worked with the League for Agrarian Reform at the time of the revolution; worked on agricultural cooperation; and worked with Chayanov on various Narkomzem projects. Was an opponent of the use of hired labour in agriculture.

Osinskii, N. (Valerian V. Obolenskii) (1887–1938), first president of the Supreme Economic Council in November 1917 and Commissar for Production. Replaced when he and others refused to support the Brest-Litovsk treaty with Germany. In the early 1920s, as Osinskii, he became deputy commissar for agriculture. In October, 1921, he suggested that Lenin name Chayanov as Narkomzem representative to Gosplan. In 1922, he was named to head the Narkomzem delegation to the Genoa conference. He was executed in 1928.

Osorgin, Mikhail Andreevich (Ilin – 1878–1942), Russian journalist and writer, used 'Osorgin' as his pen name for his most important works, but used some 50 other pseudonyms in the course of his writing career. When the First World War broke out, he was the Italian correspondent of the newspaper *Russkie Vedomosti*. In 1916, he returned to Russia, wrote a series of articles on provincial life, and returned to Petersburg just before the February Revolution in 1917. He became an editor, and contributor, to Kuskova's newspaper, *Vlast Naroda*, and in 1918 was elected vice president of the Union of Writers and president of the Union of Journalists. In 1921, he joined Kuskova and Prokopovich in the formation of the Committee to Aid the Hungry, and became editor of the *Bulletin* of that Committee. When the Committee members were arrested, he, along with Kuskova and Prokovich and three others, was sentenced to death, then exiled to Kazan. In September of 1922, he was exiled to Berlin. In 1923, he moved permanently to Paris. His most successful book, *Sivtsev Vrazhek,* was published in English as *Quiet Street.*

Parey, Paul, German publisher. He published, in German, Chayanov's book on the theory of the peasant economy, as well as several Chayanov articles on agricultural organisation.

Pasternak, Boris Leonidovich (1890–1960), poet, translator, studied music and philosophy, as well as law, at Moscow University. He was well acquainted with Germany. With his family, he visited Berlin in 1906. He enrolled at Marburg University, in 1912, to study philosophy. In August of 1922, he went to Berlin for a ten-month visit, at the time of the large Russian exhibition of art, literature and music. He mixed with Russian émigré writers and artists, as well as temporary visitors like his idol, Mayakovskii, and other friends, such as Pilniak, and read his poetry in the 'House of Arts'. Made a sentimental pilgrimage to Marburg, published several collections of his poems, including *My Sister, Life* (1922). Best known in the west for his novel, *Dr Zhivago* (1956).

Peshekhonov, Aleksei V. (1867–1933), economist, statistician, leader of the Popular (Narodnii) Socialist party; served in the Provisional government as Minister of Supply with Prokopovich; struggled with the Soviet regime and was banished from Russia in 1922. In Berlin, he joined the 'Changing Landmarks' movement, and broke with Prokopovich.

Pilnyak, Boris Andreevich (pseudonym – **Boris Vogau** – 1894–1938), began writing short stories at the age of 19, did not involve himself in the revolution, published his first novel, *The Naked Year*, in 1920, the first Russian novel about the revolution. Without knowing John Dos Passos, he used a similar 'newsreel' style of writing. He saw the revolution as a triumph for the peasantry, and, when he visited Berlin, became a central figure in the quarrel around the 'Changing Landmarks' movement.

Pozner, Vladimir, writer and poet, born in Paris, raised in Russia; became part of the turbulent literary scene before the revolution. He was among the circle of writers who called themselves 'The Serapion Brothers'. In the early 1920s, he was part of the Berlin scene of Russian émigrés and Russian visitors.

Prokopovich, Sergei Nikolaevich (1871–1955), a student at the university in Brussels, married Kuskova in 1897. Together, they joined a 'Union of Russian Social-Democrats Abroad'. At that time, they were drawn to the 'Economist' wing of the Social Democrats. When Kuskova's 'Credo' was published, they were expelled from the Social Democratic party. In 1904, they joined a 'Liberation Union', and in 1905 joined, briefly, the Cadet party – the Konstitutional Democrats. At that time, they began to publish a newspaper, called 'Untitled' (*Bez Zaglavia*).

Prokopovich had been conducting a scientific inquiry into the workers' movement, analysing the budgetary records of Petersburg's working families. These studies aroused his interest in co-operatives. In 1903, he published a small book on co-operatives which, at that time, were just beginning to become a 'movement'. Later, with the approach of war, he shifted his attention from city workers to agriculture. When a 'People's University', named for a certain General A.L. Shanyavskii, was opened in Moscow, Prokopovich joined its faculty and established a department for the study of co-operatives.

Aleksandr Chayanov, having just received his diploma from the Moscow Agricultural Institute, joined Prokopovich's secretariat. Their department quickly became the intellectual centre for the co-operative movement, and the cooperative idea became a passion on which Chayanov and Prokopovich would be forever united. In 1913, when the number of cooperative units in Russia had grown to 18,023 from only 1,625 in 1902, Prokopovich published his book on *The Cooperative Movement in Rusia, its Theory and Practice.*

In February 1917, after the collapse of the monarchy, Kuskova and Prokopovich distanced themselves from the Cadet party, and called themselves 'non-party socialists'. In April, she began to publish a newspaper, *Vlast Naroda* – The People's Authority – which covered politics in general, and the cooperative movement in particular. One of their contributors was Aleksandr Chayanov. His bibliography shows 17 contributions to the newspaper in 1917 and early 1918. The chief editor was Emmanuil Gurevich, a veteran Social Democrat and proponent of cooperatives, whose beautiful daughter, Ol'ga, would later become Chayanov's second wife. Prokopovich served as Minister of Trade and Industry, and then as Minister of Food Supply, in the ill-starred Provisional Governments. Chayanov was appointed to the post of Deputy Minister of Agriculture in the last Provisional Government, a mere week or so before the government collapsed. He never served. Kuskova and Chayanov were both members of a so-called 'Pre-Parliament' (this was another name for the Council of the Republic, created by Aleksandr Kerensky on 7 (20) October 1917, after he had declared Russia to be a Republic; the Council was to meet until a Constituent Assembly could be elected, and decide upon a new Russian government) where they spoke out on behalf of co-operatives. The Constituent Assembly was abolished by the Bolsheviks before it could conduct any business.

Chayanov, Prokopovich and Kuskova were friends, as well as colleagues. Their relationship was both academic and social. Chayanov leaned very heavily on the expertise of Prokopovich on statistical treatment of agricultural material. They both studied peasant farms and peasant farm families. At the Shaniavskii University, they consulted one another on all aspects of their teaching. They agreed on many aspects of their theoretical views.

In one area, however, they disagreed, and that disagreement was fundamental. Prokopovich was a life-long Marxist. Chayanov was an agnostic, so far as Marx was concerned. He valued Marx's work, but felt free to discard elements that appeared wrong to him. Chayanov considered Marx to be incorrect in his definition of a farmer. Marx postulated that the farmer who did not use hired labour was both an employer and an employee – in one person. Chayanov found that to be an interesting, but insupportable concept. He insisted that the farmer was neither an employer nor an employee, and that, as a consequence, without the element of wages, Marx's economic arithmetic was false. Prokopovich was unable to accept that premise, and therefore was unable to accept the foundation of Chayanov's family farm theories.

This basic disagreement did not prevent them from working together in the most friendly and fruitful manner, until Prokopovich was banished from his homeland, and Chayanov came to visit, in the guise of an employee of and adviser to the Bolshevik government. It must have been more than ironic to Prokopovich that he, the faithful Marxist, had to live in exile while Chayanov, who rejected Marxism, was accepted. Chayanov insisted that he could not understand Prokopovich's discontent with him, but he put his finger on it, in 1923, in his letter to Prokopovich [Letters 37] in which he wrote, '... if you can find it acceptable to recognize a theory of peasant farming without the idea of wages and the simple profit of capitalist thought, then all disagreements between us are easily removed ...'.

Prokopovich could not accept that. After Chayanov had left Berlin to return to Russia, Prokopovich published a book of his own, attempting to rebut all the basic elements of Chayanov's theory. The final irony is reported by Solomon, that, in 1928, when Chayanov's world was beginning to fall apart in Russia, a young Agrarian-Marxist, Ia. A. Anisimov, attacked Chayanov's theory in a series of articles and quoted, to support his attack, Prokopovich's book [*Solomon*, 1977: 134].

After the Bolshevik coup, Kuskova became a leading, and vocal opponent of the Bolshevik regime, opposing the Brest-Litovsk treaty of peace with Germany, expressing neutrality in the Civil War. When a calamitous famine struck Russia, centred in the Volga region as a result of a severe drought and widespread brush fires, she and Prokopovich set in motion the only serious effort the Bolsheviks would ever make to share a major national programme with non-Bolshevik elements of the society. The famine was the worst in Russian memory. It was caused not only by natural forces, such as drought and brush fires, but by the policies of War Communism, which had confiscated all the peasants' grain including their seed crops. Widespread destruction of agricultural areas resulted from many local peasant uprisings.

They persuaded Lenin's literary friend, Maksim Gorki, and several of Lenin's principal collaborators in the politburo, including Lev Kamenev, to support an 'All-Russian Committee for Aid to the Hungry'. Most of its members would be prominent non-communist intellectuals. Reluctantly, Lenin agreed. He nevertheless issued an order to the Politburo that 'Kuskova must be rendered strictly harmless'. He said, 'We shall get Kuskova to give us her name, her signature and a couple of carloads from those who sympathize with her. Not a thing more.' (In Lenin's words: 'Bol'she ni-che-go').

The decree authorising creation of an All-Russian Committee to Aid the Hungry, was signed on Thursday, 21 July 1921. Prokopovich and Kuskova, together with another former minister of the Provisional Government, Dr. Nikolai Kishkin, were assigned to the praesidium. In the Bolshevik files, the committee was nicknamed, in mockery of their three names: 'Prokukish'. Politburo members Kamenev [Lev Kamenev (Rozenfeld) (1883–1926)] became chairman and Aleksei Rykov [Aleksei Ivanovich Rykov (1881–1938)] became deputy chairman. Leonid Krasin , the Commissar for foreign trade, who had extensive business connections with the West, was assigned to be the official link between the non-communist committee members and the Bolshevik government.

There were some 80 members of the Committee. Chayanov and several of his economist-agronomist colleagues, including Nikolai Kondrat'iev, were among them. So was his new father-in-law, Kuskova's former editor, Emmanuil Gurevich. Chayanov and Ol'ga Gurevich were newly married. Mikhail Osorgin became editor of the Committee's own newspaper, *Pomoshch*. In addition to Gorkii, there were a number of prominent representatives of the arts and letters: Konstantin Alekseev (Stanislavskii), Aleksei Tolstoi, Anatolii Lunacharskii, Academy of Sciences president A.P. Karpinskii and vice president V.A. Staklov. Also included was 'the old revolutionary', Vera Figner.

The Committee's plan was, first, to send out appeals to the rest of the world, and second, to travel in person to major cities in Western Europe with their appeal, starting with London. Departure for London was arranged for Thursday, 18 August.

A week before their departure, Krasin went to Riga, Latvia, to meet a representative of the American Relief Administration, a prolongation of Herbert Hoover's wartime relief organisation. The American, naively, told Krasin that the ARA would provide food for the starving Russians only after the Soviet government signed a formal agreement. The story was reported in the Latvian newspaper *Sevodnia* (Today) and read by Committee members when a copy reached Moscow. Committee member N.N. Kutler , the only official of the former Tsarist government on the Committee, sighed: 'Well ... it is time for us to go home. Our work is done. Now only 35 per cent of our population will die, instead of 59 per cent, or 70 per cent.'

Lenin agreed that the Committee's work was done. He instructed the Politburo: 'Order Unshlicht (deputy chief of secret police) today with maximum speed to arrest Prokopovich and all (non-communist) members of the Committee.' On 18 August, instead of the Committee leaving for London, the arrests were carried out. A few were spared, Vera Figner among them. Prokopovich, Kuskova and four others were condemned to be shot. They survived only because Fridtjof Nansen, who had arrived to sign the agreement on behalf of the ARA, personally begged Lenin to spare them. They were exiled, instead, to Vologda, 250 miles north of Moscow, but actually settled down in a small town called Kashin.

When Kuskova and Prokopovich were allowed to return to Moscow in mid-1922, they hoped that they would be able to publish a new book on dynamic statistical analysis of the peasant economy. By this time, however, Lenin and the secret police had drawn up lists of intellectuals considered to be dangerous to the security of the Bolshevik regime. In a secret letter to GPU chief, Felix Dzerzhinskii, 19 May 1922, Lenin wrote of the intention to prepare 'exile abroad of writers and professors who are helping the counter-revolution' (Mikhail Heller in special reprint of *Pomoshch*, London, 1991). It was time, Lenin said, 'to cleanse Russia for a long time into the future'. The newspaper *Pravda*, on 2 June, carried an essay signed only by 'O.', entitled 'Dictator, Where is Thy Whip?'. The article outlined, in slightly veiled terms, Lenin's programme for the exile abroad of Russian intellectuals.

On 1 June Kuskova had already written to her friend, Vera Figner: 'Today, we leave for abroad.'

Remizov, Alexei Mikhailovich (1877–1957), short story writer, novelist, left Russia in 1922 for Berlin, went to Paris in 1923. His writing made use of *'skaz'*, the mode of speech found in semi-literate provincials. He was known for his eccentric prose, his practical jokes, his mysterious society, called 'The Great and Free Chamber of Monkeys'. In Berlin, he was one of the founders, along with Kuskova, of the 'Writer's Club'.

Rodchenko, Aleksandr Mikhailovich (1891–1956), Russian painter, photographer, illustrator and stage designer, who worked especially closely with Mayakovskii.

Rykov, Aleksei Ivanovich (1881–1938), one of Lenin's chief supporters, although when Lenin decided, shortly after the Bolshevik victory in 1917, to abandon negotiations for a coalition government with other parties, Rykov and several others resigned, temporarily. Rykov returned to Lenin's regime and succeeded Lenin as Chairman of the Council of Commissars when Lenin died. He consistently supported conservative decisions on the economy. Once, in a moment of frustration, told Stalin 'your policy doesn't even smell of economics!'. In the 1930s, Rykov and most of the other original Bolshevik leaders, were purged.

Shklovskii, Viktor Borisovich (1893–?), Russian literary figure – linguist, author, critic, innovator. Schklovskii became a central activist in the Mayakovskii – Khlebnikov – Pasternak futurist circle, and also a mentor to the writers who called themselves the 'Serapion Brothers' – Zamiatin, Kataiev, Vsevolod Ivanov, Ilf and Petrov, Zoshchenko, Pilniak and others. His political preference was the Socialist Revolutionary Party. In January of 1922, a pamphlet was published in Berlin claiming to document Socialist Revolutionary participation in a series of terrorist activities in 1918. The pamphlet was used to justify the wholesale arrest of Socialist Revolutionaries and the 'show trial' of 1922 in Moscow. Shklovskii was named in the pamphlet, and consequently had to flee for his life. He went to Berlin, where he stayed until his friends, Maksim Gorkii and Vladimir Mayakovskii, pulled the strings that permitted him to return to Russia.

Schlichter, Rudolf (1890–1955), German painter, studied art at the Academy of Karlsruhe, moved to Berlin in 1919, to join the circle of Grosz and Heartefield. In 1920, took part in the First International Dada Fair. In 1937, he was one of many German artists whose work was declared to be 'degenerate'. He was sent to prison, and, in 1942, released. He moved to Monaco, where he stayed the rest of his life.

Schlömer, Dr Friedrich translated several of Chayanov's works into German; later became a member of the International Wheat Council in London.

Smith, R.E.F. (1922–), distinguished scholar of Russian agrarian history, professor at the University of Birmingham until his retirement. Author of *The Origins of Farming in Russia* [1959], *The Enserfment of the Russian Peasant* [1968] and *Peasant Farming in Muscovy* [1977a]; co-editor, with Daniel Thorner and Basile Kerblay, of *The Theory of Peasant Economy* [*Chayanov,* 1966]. Translator of Chayanov's *Peasant Farm Organization* (in Chayanov [1966]) and of *The Journey of my Brother Alexei to the Land of Peasant Utopia* (in Smith [1977b]). It was Smith who introduced the English-speaking world to the latter.

Stresemann, Gustav (1878–1929). A monarchist, and opponent of the Weimar Republic, Stresemann, after the First World War, created his own political party, the 'German People's Party.' In June 1923, Germany's foreign minister, Walter Rathenau, was murdered by anti-Semitic terrorists. This, along with the rapidly deteriorating economy, led to a general strike of protest. The government resigned, and a 'grand coalition' of Social Democrats, German Democrats, Centre parties and Streseman's own German People's party formed a new government, with Stresemann as chancellor. Stresemann won approval for a drastic programme to stabilize the currency. After a vote of no-confidence in November, Stresemann took over the role of Foreign Minister. In the following six years, he led Germany to a reconciliation with the Western allies. In 1926, he received the Nobel Peace Prize.

Studenskii, Gennadii Aleksandrovich (1898–1930), economist, agrarian. Colleague of Chayanov. Sometimes referred to as the 'maverick' of the Organization-Production school. Arrested in 1930. Committed suicide in prison.

Sylvester (15??–1566), a priest at the Annunciation cathedral in the Kremlin, became chaplain and tutor in the court of Ivan IV. He was a member of an 'office of petitions' that would receive appeals from the people, to correct abuses of local officials. He suggested a programme of church reform. In 1560, when Ivan's wife, Anastasia, died of a mysterious illness, Sylvester was banished from the court. During his service with Ivan, he wrote and published his observations and recommendations concerning the conduct of family estates (*Domostroi*). Chayanov considered Sylvester to be the forefather of the theories of family economies. (He traced the genesis of the labour-consumer balance even deeper into history, to the bible, Chapter 16, v. 26: 'He that laboureth, laboureth for himself; for his mouth craveth it of him' [*Chayanov,* 1966: 226].)

Tatlin, Vladimir Yevgrafovich (1885– ?), artist and architect, pioneer in 1915 of Constructivism, one of the elements in the futurist-cubist movement, away from the painting of literal reality, embracing abstraction. His 'Monument to the Third International', with revolving halls and unusual lines and shapes, represented his approach to art. The Soviet government, however, did not approve of Constructivism, and his design for the monument, although internationally acclaimed, was never constructed. He worked in Russia with the Commissariat of Education as a teacher; and later worked in the theatre as a set designer.

Thorner, Daniel (1915–74), distinguished American scholar, driven out of the United States by McCarthy; after prolonged period in India, worked at the Ecole Pratique des Hautes Etudes, the Sorbonne, from 1960. Instrumental in rescuing from oblivion Chayanov's ideas in the English-speaking world by having Chayanov's major work translated into English [*Chayanov*, 1966], with the help of R.E.F. Smith and Basile Kerblay. Chayanov brought to his attention in 1952 by Zakir Husain (then Vice-Chancellor of Aligarh Muslim University, and later President of India) who came to know of Chayanov's work when doing his Ph.D. in Germany. His 'Chayanov's Concept of Peasant Economy' [1966] is valuable. Thorner's own notion of peasant economy drew on Chayanov's ideas. See, for example, Thorner [1963].

Tolstoi, Aleksei Nikolaevich (1883–1945), a distant relative of the great novelist, Count Lev Tolstoi. Aleksei, a prolific and talented writer (*Peter the First*), came to epitomise the intellectual who could accept Bolshevism but could not join the party. He was very influential with young writers.

Triolet, Elza (1897–1970), Russian author who wrote in both Russian and French,; married French poet Louis Aragon; was active in the French resistance during World War II; associated herself afterwards with the Soviet-sponsored World Peace movement. During the period 1922–24, after her separation from her first husband, she lived in Berlin; was encouraged by Gorkii to become a serious writer. After publishing several works in Russian, she began to write, with considerable success, in French. She was devoted to Mayakovskii, and saw him and many other Russian writers, poets and artists during her stay in Berlin.

Tsvetaeva, Marina Ivanovna (1892–1941), Russian poet, educated in Switzerland, Germany and France, noted for the exhilaration and passion of her work. In 1922, a firm opponent of Communism, she went to Berlin and was reunited with her husband, who had served with the White opposition to the Soviet government. They stayed in Berlin, Prague and Paris until 1938, when they returned to Russia. He was arrested and disappeared. She was exiled to the provinces, where, in 1941, she hanged herself.

Urquhart, John Leslie, chairman of the Russo-Asiatic Consolidated Corporation, the largest British-owned metallurgical and mining company in Russia before the Bolshevik revolution. He and Leonid Krasin worked together to fashion a concession agreement that would have restored much of the Russo-Asiatic operation, but the agreement failed. Urquhart frequently invited Krasin and his family to spend a weekend at the Urquhart country residence.

Ushakova, Antonina (1891–1938), typist, translator in the Danish Mission in Moscow, working for the Danish Agricultural secretary Andrei Koffod. She and Koffod, in the 1930s, were accused of being spies for England. Chayanov and Nikolai Kondrat'ev, because of their occasional meetings with Koffod, also were accused of espionage. An OGPU document stated, in addition, that Koffod and Ushakov had an inappropriate relationship with the esteemed Russian scientist, Nikolai Ivanovich Vavilov. Chayanov, Kondrat'ev and Ushakova were convicted and sentenced to death.

Ushakova, Nadezhda, artist and illustrator who used the pseudonym 'Phytopatolog U' when she did the illustrations for Chayanov's novella, *Venediktov, or Memorable Events of My Life* (1922). She was a good friend of the writer, Mikhail Bulgakov, to whom she gave a copy of Chayanov's book. Venediktov's full name was Venediktov Bulgakov. Venediktov's memorable events had to do with a dramatic visit to Moscow by Satan, in person. Students of Bulgakov, including his wife, have stated that Chayanov's book was a significant influence in the writing of Bulgakov's masterpiece, *The Master and Margarita* (first published in Moscow in 1966, long after Bulgakov's death), the plot of which also featured a visit to Moscow by Satan, in person.

Ustryalov, Nikolai (1890–1937), author of a series of articles, published under the title, *The Struggle for Russia,* stating the arguments for what came to be called the 'Changing Landmarks' movement. Ustryalov declared that the Bolshevik revolution had been essentially an expression of nationalism, with roots leading back to the Slavophiles, that the Soviets had frozen that revolution and were carrying out national tasks, and that only the Bolsheviks were capable of restoring Russia as a great power. Everyone who loved 'Mother Russia', he said, should support the Bolsheviks. Ustryalov also saw a compelling parallel with the French Revolution, and predicted that, just as in France the revolution had led to the rise of Napoleon, the next step in Russia would be the appearance of a new Emperor. He returned to Russia in 1934 and disappeared during the purges [*Raeff*, 1990: 67].

Vasnetsov, Viktor M. (1848–1926), Russian painter. He and his younger brother, Apolinarii, were associated with the group known as 'The Wanderers', and later, with the 'World of Art' movement inaugurated by Aleksandr Benois. The Vasnetsov brothers were noted for their depictions of Russian history, and Russian folk subjects.

Vikhlyaev, Panteleimon Alekseevich (1869–1928), statistician, took part in the Provisional Government in 1917; organised a statistical department at Moscow University, was the leader of the statistical cathedra at the Timiriazevskii Academy from 1920 to 1928. He worked closely with Chayanov on the subject of co-operatives, and provided statistical support for many of Chayanov's projects.

Vishnyak, Abram Grigorevich (1895–1943), editor and director of the publishing house 'Gelikon' ('Helikon'), which opened in Moscow in 1918 and moved to Berlin in 1921.

Volkoganov, Dmitri Antonovich (1928–199?), graduate of the Military-Political Academy, lieutenant-general in the army, received doctorates in philosophy and in history, author of a triptych entitled *Leaders* (*Vozhdi*) on the lives of Lenin, Trotsky and Stalin.

Vorovskii, Vatslav Vatslavovich (1871–1923), party and government publicist, carried out diplomatic assignments with several European countries. Vorovskii wrote the preface to Chayanov's utopian novel; was in line to succeed Leonid Krasin as diplomatic representative in London when he was assassinated at an international conference.

Yablonovskii, Aleksandr, contributor to the right-wing Cadet newspaper *Rul'*, completely and scathingly unsympathetic towards anyone who did not feel it a sacred duty to overthrow the Bolshevik regime in Russia. When conditions in Russian Berlin deteriorated, he moved to Paris, became a leader in the Russian Writer's Union, and worked for Milyukov on the newspaper *Poslednie Noxvosti*.

Yangirov, Rashit Marvanovich (1954 –??), studied history at Moscow University, worked as scientific associate for the Soviet Film Museum at the Union of Cinematographists. Yangirov published in the magazine *Kinostsenarii* (No.5, 1989) the text of Chayanov's film script for *Albidum – Victory over the Sun*, and accompanied the text with an account of the filming and a biography of Chayanov. The reference to the sun referred, in part, to Chayanov's scientific studies in the late 1920s, relating the power of sunshine to the growth record of various crops. The title 'Victory over the Sun' was, in addition, a deliberate reference to the futurist 'opera' a decade earlier, with the same title, and with a prologue by Khlebnikov, a libretto by Kruchenykh, music by Matiushin and sets by Malevich. It was intended to be political as well as educational and, the producers hoped, entertaining.

Yashchenko, Aleksandr Semionovich (1877–1943), Russian émigré editor of a leading émigré literary journal in Berlin, *Novaya Russkaya Kniga (NRK)*. His early education concentrated on international law, but he was drawn more strongly to philosophy, religion and literature. In 1919, he became a member of the first Soviet delegation to make an official visit to Berlin. He was the delegation's expert on international law. When his delegation returned to Moscow, Yashchenko remained in Berlin. Fellow publisher Vishnyak commented that he thus became the first Russian 'non-returnee', the Bolshevik terminology for émigrés. In Berlin, he associated himself with a group called *'Mir I Trud'*, led by Vladimir Benediktovich Stankevich; wrote for the group's newspaper, *Zhizn'*. He also wrote for the newspaper *Golos Rossii* and for the newspaper *Russkii Emigrant*. In 1921, he became associated with the American YMCA and some of its publications, but also began publication of the journal *Russkaya Kniga*, subsequently to be called *Novaya Russkaya Kniga*, which was the principal publisher in Berlin of Russian literary, scientific and economic articles.

Yesenin, Evgenii (1895–1925), and **Duncan, Isadora** (1878–1927), one of the most popular Russian poets, known for his peasant themes, and the American dancer known for her unique, sometimes shocking performances. Duncan had been conducting a dancing school in Moscow. She and Yesenin had begun an amorous relationship that led to their marriage. As newly-weds, they began a European trip that would take them, after some months, to New York. Their first stop was in Berlin, arriving on 11 May 1922, in the first commercial airline flight from Moscow. They were in Berlin until mid-June, enlivening and scandalising the city's artistic and literary world.

Zering, Professor Max (1857–1925), German economist, professor in Bonn (1885) and Berlin (1889–1925); came to know Russian agrarians during a tour of Russia by a group of German scientists in 1912.

Zherebtsov, Nikolai Tikhonovich (1882–?), studied agriculture at an institute in Kansas, became a consultant with Narkomzem and was Krasin's chief of staff in the trade mission in London.

6

Archival Sources and References

FRANK BOURGHOLTZER

ARCHIVAL SOURCES

Bakhmeteff Archive, Butler Library, Rare Books and manuscript Division, Columbia University, New York.

Baumann, Werner, 1993, 'Letter from A.V. to Professor Ernst Laur', in *Bauernstand und Burgerblock*: *Ernst Laur 1897–1918*, Zurich, Orell-Fussli Verlag [From Bibliothek des Schweiz, Bauernsekret ariats (Brugg)].

Government Archive of the Russian Federation (GARF), letters to Prokopovich and Kuskova.

Hoover Institution Archives, Nicolaevsky Collection, 'Letters from A.V. Chayanov to A.S. Yashchenko'.

Narkomzem Archive, RGAE, f478, opis I, Delo 696, List 5.

OGPU Archive, MB RF (Opened 1992). Delo R-33480. Toms 2, 10, 11, 24–29, Moskva, Case #7830/102735 (*The Toiling Peasant Party*).

'Prague Archive', GARF, F.5865, Inventory I, e.x. 548, 549, 'Letters from A.V. Chayanov to E. Kuskova and S. N. Prokopovich'.

Private Archive of A.V. Baxrax, 'Letters from A.V. Chayanov to A.V. Baxrax', excerpted in essays by Baxrax and Leonid Chertkov in *Sochinenia Botanik X*, New York: Russica.

Russian Government Library, formerly Leninka (RGB), letters to Sokrat Klepikov.

Russian Government Archive of Economy (RGAE), letter to Studenskii Chayanov Research Center (ChITs), with archive materials of Chayanov and former colleagues.

REFERENCES

Abramovitch, Raphael, 1962, *The Social Revolution, 1917–1939*, New York: International Universities Press.

Balyazin, V.N., 1990, *Professor Aleksandr Chayanov*, Moskva: Agropromizdat.

Baxrax, Aleksandr, 1980, *Po Pamyati, Po Zapisam, Literaturnye Portrety (From Memory, From Notes, Literary Portraits)*, Paris.

Baxrax, Aleksandr, 1982, *'Moi Priyatel' Botanik KH i Istoriia Parikmaxerskoi Kukly' v Istoriya Parikmaxerskoi Kuklyi i drugie Sochineniia Botanika X (Aleksandr)* ('My Buddy Botanik X in The Affair of the Hairdresser's Mannequin' and Other Works of Botanik X, [Aleksandr]), New York: Russica.

Belozerskaya-Bulgakova, Lyubov, 1983, *My Life with Mikhail Bulgakov*, Ann Arbor, MI: Ardis.

Beyer, Thomas, Gottfried Kratz and Xenia Werner, 1987, *Russian Berlin*, Berlin: Berlin Verlag.

Bortnevskii,V.G., 1993, *Russkoe Proshloe (Russian Past)*, Leningrad, Saint Petersburg: Logos.

Bulgakov, Mikhail, *Coeur de chien (Sobache Serdtse) (Heart of a Dog)*, Moscow: Raduga.

Carr, E.H., 1951, *The Bolshevik Revolution*, New York: Macmillan.

Catteau, Jacques, 1994, *La Premiere Emigration Russe*, Paris: Institut d'etudes Slaves.

Chayanov, A.V., 1921, *Opyty izucheniia isolirovannogo gosudarstva*, Moskva, Tr. Vish Seminariia, s.x. ekonomii i Politiki (*Attempts to Study the Isolated State*, Moscow, Work of High Seminar of Ag. Economy and Policy).

Chayanov A.V., 1922, *Optimalnye Razmery Zemledel'cheskikh Khoziaistv*, Moskva, Tr. Vish Seminariia s.x. ekonomii i Politika (*Optimal Size of an Agricultural Enterprise*, Moscow, Work of High Seminar of Ag. Economy and Policy).

Chayanov, A.V., 1931, *Uchet i Metody Opredeleniia Effektivnosti Sotsialisticheskogo Xoziaistva i Zemledeliia*, Moskva (*Calculation and Methods of Determining the Effectiveness of Socialist Agriculture*), Moscow). Unpublished manuscript in Arkhiv MB RFD R33480. T.11 L.171a.

Chayanov, A.V., 1966, *On The Theory of Peasant Economy*, Homewood, IL: Richard Irwin, Inc. (American Economic Association). Edited by Daniel Thorner, Basile Kerblay and R.E.F. Smith.

Chayanov, A.V., 1982, *Istoriia Parikmaxerskoi Kukly i drugya Sochinenya Botanika KH (Aleksandr Chayanov)* (*The Affair of the Hairdresser's Mannequin and Other Works of Botanik X [Aleksandr Chayanov]*), New York: Russica

Chayanov, Alexander, 1991, *The Theory of Peasant Co-operatives*, London and New York: I.B. Tauris. With an Introduction by Viktor Danilov.

Chayanov, A.V. and G. Studenskii, 1922, *Istoriia Biudzhetnyx Isledovaniia* (*History of Budget Research*), Moscow.

Chayanov, A.V. and S.A. Klepikov, S.A. (red.), 1922, 'Statisticheskii Spravochnik po Agrarnoma Voprosu', Moskva, Novaia Derevnia, Vyp 3 ('Statistical Reference on Agrarian Questions', Moscow, New Countryside, Issue 3).

Chayanov, V.A., 1998, *A.V. Chayanov - Chelovek, Uchenyi, Grazhdanin*

(*A.V. Chayanov – the Man, the Scholar, the Citizen*), Moscow: Press of MSXA.

Chayanov, V.A., and A.V. Petrikov, 1998, 'A.V. v Sledstvii OGPU po Delu Trudovoi Krestianskoi Partii 1930-1932 gg' *v Almanax Selskii Mir*, Moskva, Mart 1998. ('A.V. Chayanov in the OGPU Investigation, in the Case of the Toiling Peasant Party, Years 1930–1932', in *Almanac of the World of Agriculture*, Moscow, March 1998.)

Chayanova, Ol'ga, 1925, *Torzhestvo Muz* (*Celebration of The Muse*), Moscow: Press of M and S Sabashnikov.

Chernov, Victor, 1936, *The Great Russian Revolution*, New Haven, CT: Yale University Press.

Chertkov, Leonid, 1982, *'A.V.Chaiynov kak Prozaik' v Istoriia Parikmaxerskoi Kuklyi i Drugie Sochineniia Botanika X (Aleksandr)* (*'A.V. Chayanov as a Prose Writer' in The Affair of the Hairdresser's Mannequin and Other Works of Botanik X* [Aleksandr Chayanov]), New York: Russica.

Cox, Terry and Gary Littlejohn, 1984, *Kritsman and the Agrarian Marxists*, London: Frank Cass.

Crankshaw, Edward, 1976, *The Shadow of the Winter Palace*, New York: The Viking Press.

Danilov, Viktor, 1991, Introduction: 'Alexander Chayanov as a Theoretician of the Co-operative Movement', in Alexander Chayanov, *The Theory of Peasant Cooperatives*, London and New York: I.B. Tauris.

Durrenberger, E. Paul, 1984, *Chayanov, Peasants and Economic Anthropology*, Orlando, FL: Academic Press.

Fischer, Louis, 1964, *The Life of Lenin*, New York: Harper & Rowe.

Fleishman, L., Hughes, R. and O. Raevsky-Hughes, 1983, *Russkii Berlin*, Paris: YMCA.

Geller, Mikhail, 1991, 'O Golode, Xlebe i Sovetskoi Vlasti', *Pomoshch, Byulleten Vserossiiskogo Komiteta Pomoshshi Golodaiushchim*, ('On Hunger, Bread and Soviet Power', *Help, Bulletin of the All Russian*

Committee to Help the Hungry), 1921, No. 1/3, London: Overseas Publications, Interchange.

Heller, Mikhail, 1986, *Utopia in Power*, New York: Summit Books Overseas Publication Interchange Press.

Karpova, Rosa Fedorovna, 1962, *L.B. Krasin, Sovetskii Diplomat (L.B. Krasin, Soviet Diplomat)*, Moscow: Press of Soc. Econ. Literature.

Kennan, George F., 1961, *Russia and the West Under Lenin and Stalin*, London: Hutchinson.

Kerblay, Basile H., 1966., 'A.V. Chayanov: Life, Career, Works', in A.V. Chayanov *On The Theory of Peasant Economy*, Homewood, IL: Richard Irwin (American Economic Association).

Kerensky, Alexander, 1965, *Russia and History's Turning Point*, London: Cassell.

Koen, Stiven, 1988, *Bukharin, Politicheskaia Biografiia 1888–1938* (Steven Cohen, *Bukharin, Political Biography 1888–1938*), Moskva: Progress.

Kondrat'ev, N.D., 1991, 'Osnovnye Problemy Ekonomicheskoi Statiki i Dinamiki', v *Serii Sotsiologicheskoe Nasledye* ('Basic Problems of Economic Statistics and Dynamics', in *Series of Sociological Heritage*), Moscow: Press of Nauka.

Krassin, Lubov, [no date], *Leonid Krassin: His Life and Work*, London: Skeffington.

Kremnev, Ivan (Chayanov), 1920, *Puteshestvie Moego Brata Alekseya v Stranu Krest'yanskoi Utopii*, Predel Orlovskogo, P. (Vorovskogo V) (*The Journey of my Brother Aleksei to the Land of Peasant Utopia*, Foreword by P. Orlovskii (V. Vorovskii), Moscow: Government Press.

Kuskova, E.D., 1928, 'Mesiats "Soglashatelstva"' ('Month of "Compromise"') *Volya Rossii (Russia's Freedom)*, No.3, Prague.

Leont'ev, Ya.V., 1993, 'Likvidatsiya VSERPOMGOLa', v *Russkoe Proshloe*, 4, pp.330–42, Sovietsko-Amerikanskoe Predpriiatie 'Svelen', Leningrad ('Liquidation of VSERPOMGOL', in *Russia's Past*, 4, pp.330–42, Soviet-American Enterprise 'Svelen', Leningrad).

Lewin, Moshe, 1975, *Russian Peasants and Soviet Power*, New York: W.W. Norton.

Medvedev, Roy A., 1971, *Let History Judge*, New York, Knopf.

Medvedev. Zhores, 1987, *Soviet Agriculture*, New York and London: W.W. Norton.

Murav'ev, Vladimir Bronislavovich, 1989, *Chayanov, A.V., Povesti, Primechaniya* (*Chayanov, A.V., Tales, Notes*), Moscow: Sovremennik.

Nikonov, Aleksandr Aleksandrovich (ed.), 1989, *A.V. Chaianov, Krestianskoe Khoziaistvo,* Moscow: Ekonimika in the series *Ekonmicheskoe Nasledie* (*Economic Legacy*).

O'Connor, Timothy Edward, 1992, *The Engineer of Revolution, L.B. Krasin and the Bolsheviks*, Boulder, CO and Oxford: Westview Press.

Osorgin, Mikhail A., 1982, *Selected Stories, Reminiscences, and Essays* (Edited, translated and commented by D.M. Fiene), Ann Arbor, MI: Ardis.

Prokopovich, S.N., 1913, *Kooperativnoe Dvizhenie v Rossii, ego Teoriya i Praktika* (*Cooperative Movement in Russia, its Theory and Practice*), Moscow: M and S Sabashchnikov.

Raeff, Marc, 1990, *Russia Abroad*, New Yor and Oxford: Oxford University Press.

Savitskii, Petr; Suvchinskii, P.P. and Kn. N.S., Trubetskii, 1923, *Evraziiskii Vremennik* (Eurasian Vremennik), Berlin: Eurasian Book Publishers.

Serova, Evgenia, 1988, 'Sochetanie form Kooperatsii v Uchenii A.V. Chayanov i Kooperativnoe Stroitelstvo v S.S.S.R', *Vesti s-x Nauki*, No.11 (387) ('Combination of Forms of Cooperation in the Teaching of A.V. Chayanov and Cooperative Construction in the U.S.S.R', *News of Agricultural Science*, No.11, 387).

Shelestov, Dmitrii, 1990, *Vremya Alekseya Rykova* (*The Time of Aleksei Rykov*), Moscow: Progress.

Shklovskii, Viktor, 1970, *A Sentimental Journey*, Ithaca, NY and London: Cornell University Press.

Smith, R.E.F., 1959, *The Origins of Farming in Russia*, Paris: Mouton.

Smith, R.E.F., 1968, *The Enserfment of the Russian Peasant*, London and New York: Cambridge University Press.

Smith, R. E. F., 1977a, *Peasant Farming in Muscovy*, Cambridge: Cambridge University Press.

Smith, R.E.F. (ed.), 1977b, *The Russian Peasant: 1980 and 1984*, London: Frank Cass. Published originally as a special issue of *The Journal of Peasant Studies*, Vol.4, No.1. This contains Smith's translation of Chayanov's *The Journey of my Brother Alexei to the Land of Peasant Utopia*.

Smith, R.E.F., 1981, 'Nesko'lko Slov ob Istochnikakh Romana G. Orvella "1984"' ('A Few Words About the Sources of the Novel of G. Orwelll, 1984'), (Ssylki, vstrechauiushchiesia v Tekste Etoi Stati, Otnosyatsya k Spetsial'nomi Izdaniiu (Quotations occurring in the Special Issue of): in *The Journal of Peasant Studies*, Vol.4, No.l, Oct.1976; in Kremnev, Iv. (A. Chayanov), *Puteshestvie moego brata Alekseya v Stranu Krest'yanskoi Utopii* (*The Journey of my Brother Alexeii to the Land of Peasant Utopia*), New York: Silver Age.

Smith, R.E.F., Daniel Thorner and Basile Kerblay, 1966, 'Preface', in A.V. Chayanov *On The Theory of Peasant Economy*, Homewood, IL: Richard Irwin (American Economic Association).

Solomon, Susan Gross, 1977, *The Soviet Agrarian Debate*, Boulder, CO: Westview Press.

Solomon, Susan Gross, 1993, *Beyond Sovietology*, Armonk, NY: M.E. Sharpe.

Stalin, J., 1930, 'Political Report to the Sixteenth Party Congress of the Russian Communist Party', in *Kommunisticheskaia partiya Sovestskogo Soiuza, Tsentralnyi komitet* (*The Communist Party of the Soviet Union, Central Committee*), New York: Library Publishers.

The Great Soviet Enclycopedia, 1st edn, Vol.17 [cited in *Abramovitch*, 1962].

Thorner, Daniel, 1963, 'Peasant Economy as a Category in Economic History', *The Economic Weekly*, Special Number, July, Vol.XV, Nos.28–29-30. Published also in *Second International Conference of Economic History, Aix-en-Provence, 1962*, The Hague: Mouton, 1965. Reprinted in Thorner [1980].

Thorner, Daniel, 1965, 'A Post-Marxian Theory of Peasant Economy: The School of A.V. Chayanov', *The Economic Weekly*, Annual Number, Feb., Vol.XVII, Nos.5–6–7. This was reprinted subsequently as Thorner [1966]. Reprinted in Thorner [1980].

Thorner, Daniel, 1966, 'Chayanov's Concept of Peasant Economy', in A.V. Chayanov, *On The Theory of Peasant Economy*, Homewood, IL, Richard Irwin (American Economic Association).

Thorner, Daniel, 1980, *The Shaping of Modern India*, New Delhi: Allied Publishers for the Sameeksha Trust.

Trubetskoy, Nikolai Sergeevich, 1991, *The Legacy of Genghis Khan*, Ann Arbor, MI: Slavic Publications

Volkogonov, Dmitri, 1994a, *Lenin: A New Biography*, New York: The Free Press (Simon & Schuster).

Volkogonov, Dmitrii, 1994b, *Lenin: Politicheskii Portret v dvux knigax (Lenin: A Political Portrait in Two Volumes)*, Moscow: Novosti.

Willett, John, 1978, *Art and Politics in the Weimar Period*, New York: Pantheon Books.

Yangirov, Rashit Marvanovich, 1989, 'K Istorii Odnoi Kinoutopii', *v Kinostsenarii* 5, 1989, pp.154–63. ('To the History of a Cine-Utopia', in *Kinoscenarios* 5, 1989, pp.154–63.)

Zaslavskaya, Tatyana, 1990, *The Second Socialist Revolution*, London: I.B. Tauris.

www.ingramcontent.com/pod-product-compliance
Ingram Content Group UK Ltd.
Pitfield, Milton Keynes, MK11 3LW, UK
UKHW041840280225
455677UK00010B/263